BIG IDEA'S

VeggieTales®

Bible ATLAPEDIA

BIG IDEA'S
VeggieTales®

Bible ATLAPEDIA

by Cindy Kenney

INTEGRITY®
PUBLISHERS
family
Nashville

www.bigidea.com

www.integritypublishers.com

VeggieTales Bible Atlapedia

Copyright © 2006 by Big Idea, Inc.
Illustrations copyright © 2006 by Big Idea, Inc.
Photography copyright © 2006 by Zev Radovan (www.biblelandpictures.com)

Published by Integrity Publishers, a division of Integrity Media, Inc., 660 Bakers Bridge Ave, Suite 200, Franklin, TN 37067.

HELPING PEOPLE WORLDWIDE EXPERIENCE the MANIFEST PRESENCE of GOD

Written by: Cindy Kenney
Design by: John Trent and Big Idea Design

ISBN 10: 1-59145-447-6
ISBN 13: 978-1-59145-447-2

Printed in the United States of America
06 07 08 09 QBR 9 8 7 6 5 4 3 2 1

Table of Contents

Section 1: Introduction.................................... 7

Section 2: Books of the Bible...................... 16

Section 3: Bible Timeline........................... 86

Section 4: People of the Bible.................. 100

Section 5: Bible Life and Times.............. 126

Section 6: Bible Maps................................. 144

Dear Bob and Larry,

I have some questions for you about the Bible. I'm one of the best readers in my second grade class. I've read A LOT of books. But I just don't understand the Bible. It has so many pages and it's really confusing. I asked my friend Pete (he's in the third grade) and he said the Bible is just for grown ups.

Is that true? And if it's not true, and the Bible is supposed to be for kids too, can you help me understand all the stuff that's in it?

Thank you very much.

Katy Crocket
Detroit, Michigan

Dear Larry and Bob,

How do all the grown-ups know where to find things in the Bible? The minister doesn't tell them a page number, he says a name and some other numbers and they all just know what page he's talking about. Can you tell me how they do this?

Thanks,

Lyle Berger
Vero Beach, FL

P.S. I drew this picture of LarryBoy for you, he's my favorite!

Hi Kids!

Wow, these are great questions. And these letters are just two of the many that we've received asking about the Bible. We get letters all the time asking questions like: Who wrote the Bible? Where did the stories in the Bible take place? And why should we read the Bible? So we decided to answer these questions once and for all.

But Larry and I knew we couldn't do this one alone. No way! So we asked all our VeggieTales friends to help us.

We call our project the VeggieTales Atlapedia!

That's because it's part Atlas and part Encyclopedia!

Atlas (at·las) noun: a book of maps, sometimes with supplementary illustrations and graphic analyses. *(Pa Grape, I believe, is supplying the supplementary analyses!)*

Encyclopedia (en·cy·clo·pe·di·a) noun: a reference work containing articles on numerous aspects of a particular field.

Books of the Bible

Larry and I will begin our Atlapedia at the beginning! We'll tell you how God created this whole library of books inside just one big book, the Bible. AND we'll tell you what each book is about and what some of the stories mean.

Bible Timeline

Section three of our Atlapedia will feature a brand-new invention from Pa Grape. It's a time machine that starts at the very beginning of the Bible, when God created the world. It will put hundreds of years of stories and people in order for you! It's a big help. Pa named his invention J.I.M.M. We don't know why.

People of the Bible

Archibald Asparagus spent hours and hours in the research stacks of the Bumblyburg Library pouring through volumes of old, dusty books so that he could tell you all about the people in the Bible. The people in the Bible lived a very long time ago and some of them did some pretty amazing things! Archibald can't wait to share all the great things he learned. He's still a little dusty from the research, but that won't bother you from where you're sitting.

[David]
Reaching into his bag and taking out a stone,
he slung it and struck the Philistine on the forehead.
The stone sank into his forehead,
and he fell facedown on the ground.
1 Samuel 17:49

Bible Life and Times

Jimmy and Jerry got the difficult assignment of researching how all the people lived during Bible times. They learned all about what the people wore, what kind of jobs they had, what kind of houses they lived in, and, most importantly to the Gourd brothers, what kind of food they ate. I'm sure you'll find their chapter to be quite interesting... and tasty too!

Maps of the Bible

The Pirates Who Don't Do Anything finally agreed to do something for our Atlapedia! They weren't very excited about the idea at first. But when they could sail the seven seas tasting cheese curls from around the world, they hoisted the sails and off they went! In their section you'll find all the maps that will help you see where in the world all these great things happened.

LET'S GET

So here it is, Katy and Lyle, and all the other kids who have written us over the years with questions about the Bible. We hope you enjoy our VeggieTales Atlapedia . . . and we hope it helps answer some questions too!

STARTED!

THE BIBLE DOES WHAT?

WHAT IS THE BIBLE?

That's the most important question, and the one we will answer first. The Bible is a message from God. It was written a long time ago by many different people whom God chose to do the job. He inspired them, or guided them to record just the right infomation. So everything we read in the Bible is stuff that God wants us to know.

We know that we can always trust what it says. And it is all there to help us know how to build our faith in him. The Bible is for anyone, young or old, who wants to learn about God.

THAT'S A LOT OF INFORMATION!

Yes, but there is a very easy way to help you find your way around the Bible:

— There are **SIXTY-SIX BOOKS** in the Bible. Each one has a different name.

— Every one of these sixty six books is divided into a different section called a **CHAPTER**.

— Every chapter is sub-divided into a smaller section called a **VERSE**. Verses can be several words long to one or two complete sentences in length.

— Here is a sample Bible verse: **JOHN 3:16**

Can you find it in your Bible? First look up the **BOOK**. (John) Then find the big **CHAPTER** number (3). Then go to the correct **VERSE** number, which is printed smaller than the chapter number (16).

Great! Now we're ready to start learning about each of the books in the Bible!

THe OLD TeSTAMenT

The book of Genesis tells a lot about what God is like. God is awesome and powerful. God wants his people to obey him. But God also promises to forgive, help, and protect, even when we sin and do things wrong.

MAJOR EVENTS:

GENESIS Scroll;
Fragment found in Qumran,
dated 1st century A.D. Text contains
the first two passages of the story of creation.

genesis
Creation, Sin, and Forgiveness

AUTHOR:
Tradition says Moses.

KEY SCRIPTURE:
So God created man in his own image, in the image of God he created them; male and female he created them. *Genesis 1:27*

WHAT THIS BOOK IS ABOUT:
The very first book of the Bible is Genesis. It starts at the beginning of time. It tells all about how God created the earth and everything in it. God made people like him in many ways. God also made each person unique and special.

God Creates the World:
The Bible says God created the entire world in six days and rested on the seventh day.

• **Day 1:** God creates the heaven and the earth. He creates light and calls it day; he creates darkness and calls it night.

• **Day 2:** God separates the waters from the sky.

• **Day 3:** God separates the water from dry land. God creates vegetation and plants with seeds and fruits.

• **Day 4:** God creates the seasons, days, and years. He creates the sun, the moon, and the stars.

• **Day 5:** God creates living creatures: birds in the sky and fish in the sea.

• **Day 6:** God creates animals on the land. Then God creates people in his image.

• **Day 7:** God sees everything that he has made and calls it very good. He rests from his work. Then he blesses the seventh day and makes it holy. *(Genesis 1:1 thru 2:3)*

Adam and Eve;
Silver cover from 18th-century Polish prayer book

Adam and Eve: Adam and Eve were the very first two people God created. God created them without any sin and placed them in a beautiful place called the Garden of Eden that had everything that they could ever need! But God asked them not to eat from the tree in the center of the garden.

Satan tempted Adam and Eve to disobey God by eating from the tree. When they did, God was very angry and disappointed. God told Adam and Eve that people would be punished for their choice. *(Genesis 2:4 thru 3:24)*

Cain and Abel: These two brothers were sons of Adam and Eve. Cain made a terrible choice to kill his brother, Abel. *(Genesis 4)*

Noah and the great flood: People chose to disobey God more and more. God was very sad about all of this, but he was angry too! So he decided to punish the people for their sin.

God found one person who was a good and honorable man: Noah. God told Noah to build a huge boat called an ark. Then God told Noah to bring his family onto the boat, along with every kind of animal. It rained for forty days and forty nights until the rain covered the entire earth.

When the earth began to dry up, God placed a rainbow in the sky as a promise that he would never destroy the earth and people with a flood again! *(Genesis 6–9)*

The Tower of Babel: Everyone in the world spoke just one language. The people decided to build a city with an enormous tower that reached all the way to heaven! But as they worked on the tower, the people became filled with pride. God doesn't want people to worship themselves! So God gave the people different languages. When that happened, the people stopped building the tower, because they couldn't understand each other any longer. *(Genesis 11:1 thru 11:9)*

Abraham's Faith: There was a faithful man named Abram. God promised Abram he would have a big family. Abram's name was changed to Abraham, and God selected him to be father

Noah's Ark;
The dove is returning with a branch in its beak. A sign that the flood water has receded. Hebrew manuscript from North France, dating 1280.

of the nation Israel! Abraham was one hundred years old and his wife Sarah was ninety when they had a baby they named Isaac.

God tested Abraham's faith by asking him to sacrifice his son. Abraham obeyed God, but God didn't really want any harm to come to Isaac, so God saved the boy. *(Genesis 12:1 thru 25:18)*

Isaac and Rebekah: Isaac was the promised son born to Abraham and Sarah. He married Rebekah, and they had twin boys, Jacob and Esau. *(Genesis 21–35)*

Joseph Being Sold by His Brothers;
Illustration from the Golden Hagada, dated 1320

Jacob and Esau: Jacob and Esau were twins, but they were very different. Esau was red and hairy and a great hunter. Jacob preferred to stay at home and work around the house or care for the flocks in the field. One day, Jacob was home cooking stew when Esau returned from hunting. He was so hungry that he sold his inheritance to Jacob for a bowl of stew. *(Genesis 25:19 thru 36:43)*

Jacob has twelve sons: Jacob's twelve sons were Reuben, Simeon, Levi, Judah, Issachar, Zubulun, Dan, Naphtali, Gad, Asher, Joseph, and Benjamin. Jacob's sons became the leaders over all the parts of Israel. Joseph was Jacob's favorite son. Joseph received a beautiful coat of many colors from his dad, which made his brothers very jealous. *(Genesis 37:12–23)*

Joseph's faithfulness and forgiveness: Joseph was always faithful and obedient to God. His brothers sold him into slavery, he had many hard years, and he was even wrongly put into jail. Because Joseph had faith and always did what was right in God's eyes, he became the second most important man in all of Egypt! When there was no food in Israel, Joseph's brothers came to him to ask for food. Joseph helped his brothers and forgave them. *(Genesis 37–50)*

Hey Jude!

When my brother, Jude, threw me into the mineshaft, it was the worst day of my life. But what he intended for harm, God used for good. You can always trust God, even on the really bad days.

Exodus and Crossing of the Red Sea;
Wall painting from the Dura Europos, dated 245 A.D.

exodus
The Great Escape!

AUTHOR:
Tradition says Moses.

KEY SCRIPTURE:
The Lord said, "I have indeed seen the misery of my people in Egypt. I have heard them crying out because of their slave drivers, and I am concerned about their suffering. So I have come down to rescue them from the hand of the Egyptians and to bring them up out of that land into a good and spacious land, a land flowing with milk and honey." *Exodus 3:7–8*

WHAT THIS BOOK IS ABOUT:
Exodus means "going out," which is what the book is all about. The number of Israelite people grew in large numbers, and the Egyptians were afraid that they would take over the land! So the Egyptians overpowered the Israelites and made them their slaves.

Moses was chosen by God to lead the people out of slavery and into a wonderful land that God promised them. Then God gave Moses the Ten Commandments as laws for everyone to live by.

As Moses was on Mount Sinai getting the commandments, the people got tired of waiting. They lost faith in God and worshiped idols. This made God angry, so he made them wander in the desert for many years.

The book of Exodus shows God's willingness to come to our rescue, but it also shows the importance of doing what God asks us to do.

MAJOR EVENTS:
The Israelites were slaves in Egypt: When God's people grew in number, it worried the Egyptians because they were afraid that the Israelites would take over the land. So, the Egyptians made the Israelites their slaves for four hundred years as the Israelites cried out to God to save them. *(Exodus 1:1 thru 12:30)*

Baby Moses: When Moses was born, his sister and mother sent him down the river in a basket to save him from evil. The Egyptian king's daughter found Moses and raised him in the palace.

God appeared to Moses in a burning bush: God spoke to Moses in the form of a fiery bush and told him to lead his people out of slavery in Egypt. *(Exodus 3:1 thru 4:17)*

The plagues and Passover: Moses and his brother, Aaron, appeared before the Pharaoh (the Egyptian king) and told him that God said to free his people from slavery. But Pharaoh did not listen. So God gave Moses the power to send ten different plagues upon Egypt to show Pharaoh his amazing power.

The plagues were: turning all the water into blood; plagues of frogs, lice, swarms of flies; death of the livestock; boils that appeared on the skin; a huge hail storm; locusts that swarmed the land; and the ninth plague was a darkness that covered the earth for three full days. The Egyptians were devastated by all the plagues, and Pharaoh was angry. But Moses told him there would be one final plague—the death of every firstborn son of the Egyptians. *(Exodus 7:14 thru 12:33)*

Moses Receiving the Ten Commandments on Mt. Sinai; Illustration from the Sarajevo Hagada, 14th century

The exodus and crossing of the Red Sea: After the last plague, Pharaoh finally let the people go, and the people fled from Egypt to the promised land by God. But Pharaoh came after them again! The people were trapped in front of the Red Sea! But God had Moses part the waters so the people could cross. Then the sea came crashing down on the Egyptians and the Israelites were safe at last. *(Exodus 12:31 thru 14:31)*

The Ten Commandments:

Moses led the Israelites to Sinai where God gave him the Ten Commandments:

1. I am the Lord your God, who brought you out of Egypt, out of the land of slavery. You shall have no other gods before me. You shall not make for yourself an image in the form of anything in heaven above or on the earth beneath or in the waters below. You shall not bow down to them or worship them; for I, the Lord your God, am a jealous God, punishing the children for the sin of the parents to the third and fourth generation of those who hate me, but showing love to a thousand generations of those who love me and keep my commandments.

2. You shall not misuse the name of the Lord your God, for the Lord will not hold anyone guiltless who misuses his name.

3. Remember the Sabbath day by keeping it holy. Six days you shall labor and do all your work, but the seventh day is a Sabbath to the Lord your God. On it you shall not do any work, neither you, nor your son or daughter, nor your male or female servant, nor your animals, nor any foreigner residing in your towns. For in six days the Lord made the heavens and the earth, the sea, and all that is in them, but he rested on the seventh day. Therefore the Lord blessed the Sabbath day and made it holy.

4. Honor your father and your mother, so that you may live long in the land the Lord your God is giving you.

5. You shall not murder.

6. You shall not commit adultery.

7. You shall not steal.

8. You shall not give false testimony against your neighbor.

9. You shall not covet your neighbor's house.

10. You shall not covet your neighbor's wife, or his male or female servant, his ox or donkey, or anything that belongs to your neighbor. *(Exodus 20:1–17)*

Dead Sea Scroll;
Fragment of a parchment found in the Judean desert. Text is from Leviticus, chapters 23 and 24.

Be Holy

AUTHOR:

Tradition says Moses.

KEY SCRIPTURE:

Be holy because I, the LORD your God, am holy. *Leviticus 19:2*

WHAT THIS BOOK IS ABOUT:

Leviticus means "and he called," which meant the people of Israel were called by God to do something very special. God led his people out of Egypt and gave them his laws. For two years those people lived at the foot of Mount Sinai to learn about God's holiness and how to worship him.

MAJOR EVENTS:

Rules for worship: God gave his people important rules for holy worship. The entire book shows how God taught the people to be holy and follow him. The people learned about sacrifice, offering, thankfulness, praise, and forgiveness. *(Leviticus 1–17)*

Rules for living: God wanted the Israelites to understand how to live a holy life. God especially wanted his people to know how to have a closer relationship to him. *(Leviticus 18–27)*

numbers
Desert Wandering

AUTHOR:
Tradition says Moses.

KEY SCRIPTURE:
The LORD bless you and keep you; the LORD make his face shine upon you and be gracious to you; the LORD turn his face toward you and give you peace. *Numbers 6:24–26*

WHAT THIS BOOK IS ABOUT:
The book of Numbers tells the story of how God's people wandered in the desert for years. While they were there, the government took a census to find out the total number of Israelites that were there. That's how the title of this book was chosen.

MAJOR EVENTS:
The Israelites prepare for travel: God gave the Israelites rules for how to worship and live as they traveled toward the land of Canaan. *(Numbers 1:1 thru 10:10)*

Grumble, Grumble, Grumble: The Israelites did not have much faith in God, and they complained a lot! So God did not feel they were ready to go to the Promised Land. He made them live in the desert for another forty years. Moses sent twelve spies into Canaan, and they reported back that the people there were too strong for the Israelites to overpower. But two spies, Joshua and Caleb, disagreed. They felt God would help them take over the land. *(Numbers 10:11 thru 14:45; 15:1 thru 21:35)*

Balaam and a talking donkey: Balaam believed in God, but he was also greedy. He disobeyed

Desert of Zin;
*In Central Negev from where Moses sent the spies into Canan (**Numbers 13:21**)*

The Promised Land;
The Veggies sing about the Promised Land in "Josh and the Big Wall"

God because he wanted many riches. The donkey that Balaam was riding spoke to him and saved him from an angel with a sword. Balaam asked for God's forgiveness and then he blessed the Israelites. *(Numbers 22:5–40)*

Be Faithful

AUTHOR:

Tradition says Moses and Joshua.

KEY SCRIPTURE:

Love the LORD your God with all your heart and with all your soul and with all your strength. These commandments that I give you today are to be upon your hearts. Impress them on your children. Talk about them when you sit at home and when you walk along the road, when you lie down and when you get up. Tie them as symbols on your hands and bind them on your foreheads. Write them on the doorframes of your houses and on your gates. *Deuteronomy 6:5–9*

WHAT THIS BOOK IS ABOUT:

Deuteronomy means "second law," because it explains the laws God gave to Moses and the Israelites at Mt. Sinai. Many of those laws are repeated in this book.

God wants his people to remember how much he loves them. God shows the people that he is a powerful God and he will punish the people when they disobey him. God wants his people to trust him and stay strong in their faith.

Mt. Nebo;
Memorial commemorating the place from which Moses saw the land of Canaan

JOSHUA
The Promised Land

AUTHOR:
Unknown, likely Joshua

KEY SCRIPTURE:
Be very careful to keep the commandment and the law that Moses the servant of the LORD gave you: to love the LORD your God, to walk in all his ways, to obey his commands, to hold fast to him and to serve him with all your heart and with all your soul. *Joshua 22:5*

WHAT THIS BOOK IS ABOUT:
The book of Joshua shows how God guided the people into the Promised Land. Joshua, Moses' right-hand-man, was a fierce and faithful military commander. Moses appointed him the leader of God's people when he died. Joshua and Caleb were the only people who survived slavery in Egypt and entered the Promised Land.

After the people crossed the river, they arrived at Jericho for their first battle. With God's help, they won many battles.

MAJOR EVENTS:
Remembering what God has done: Moses reminded the people of God's awesome power and love. He reminded them about how God helped them out of slavery. *(Deuteronomy 1:4 thru 4:43)*

Remembering God's rules: Moses reminded the people of God's Ten Commandments that teach us how to live like God wants us to. Moses gave the people many laws for worship, ruling the nation, daily living, and how to treat one another. *(Deuteronomy 4:44 thru 28:68)*

Called to be faithful: Moses told the people to be holy and faithful. Moses encouraged the people to keep their commitments to God with all their hearts, souls, minds, and strength. *(Deuteronomy 29–30)*

Moses died: God let Moses see Canaan from the top of Mt. Nebo before he died at the age of 120. Moses appointed Joshua as the new leader to take the people into the Promised Land. *(Deuteronomy 31)*

Joshua's Tomb;
Traditional site of the tomb of Joshua in Northern Galilee

Keep Walking!

"Keep walking but you won't knock down our wall. Keep walking, but she isn't going to fall. It's plain to see that your brains are very small to think walking will be knocking down our wall."

Joshua divided the land into twelve tribal areas. He encouraged the people to love, obey, and follow the one and only God.

MAJOR EVENTS:

Joshua and the battle of Jericho: Joshua was chosen to lead God's people after the death of Moses. When they faced their first battle at Jericho, God helped Joshua and told the people to march around the walls once a day for six days. On the seventh day, they did it seven times. The priests blew trumpets and the people shouted and the walls came down! *(Joshua 1–12)*

A woman named Rahab: Joshua sent spies into Jericho before the Israelite army arrived. A woman named Rahab opened her home and hid the spies while they were there. They promised Rahab that she would be safe, so when the battle of Jericho was over, Rahab and her family were saved. *(Joshua 2:1 thru 6:25)*

The twelve tribes of Israel: Before Joshua died, he divided the land and gave it to twelve tribes so they could create their new homes. He appointed judges to help the people with their problems and encouraged them to be faithful and obedient to the Lord. *(Joshua 13–24)*

JUDGES
God's Leaders

AUTHOR:
Unknown

KEY SCRIPTURE:
The Israelites did evil in the eyes of the LORD; they forgot the LORD their God and served the Baals and the Asherahs. *Judges 3:7*

WHAT THIS BOOK IS ABOUT:
After Joshua's death, the people did not have a strong leader to keep them faithful to God. So they began doing things their own way and once again disobeyed God.

Samson Destroying the Philistine Temple;
Illustration from a 15th-century Bible, France

Sadly, the people started to worship gods of their own and turned to a life of sin. This made God angry, and it was up to the judges to help. The judges were not perfect people, but they did their best to be loyal and faithful to God. They depended on God to help them lead his people.

MAJOR EVENTS:

Israel is disobedient: As Israel settled into their new land, the people lost faith again! The people did many things wrong. Still, they cried out to God for help, and he responded with love. (Judges 1:1 thru 3:6)

The judges come to the rescue: Even though God helped the people, they also paid for their sins. They were punished for what they did wrong. When the people were ready to return to God, he chose some interesting leaders to help.

The Judges of Israel were: Othniel *(Judges 3:7–11)*; Ehud *(Judges 3:12–30)*; Shamgar *(Judges 3:31)*; Deborah *(Judges 4–5)*; Gideon *(Judges 6–8)*; Tola *(Judges 10:1–2)*; Jair *(Judges 10:3–5)*; Jephthah *(Judges 10:6–12:7)*; Ibzan *(Judges 12:8–10)*; Elon *(Judges 12:11–12)*; Abdon *(Judges 12:13–15)*; and Samson *(Judges 13–16)*. *(Judges 3:7 thru 21:25)*

Deborah: God sent Deborah to help Barak fight the Canaanites with their many chariots. Deborah went with him and the Canaanites were defeated! *(Judges 4:4 thru 5:15)*

Gideon: An angel appeared to a farmer named Gideon and told him to save Israel. He asked for a sign from God, and God gave the sign to him. Then Gideon gathered a huge army to fight the Midianites, but God told Gideon he had too many men! Gideon had to send the entire army home, except for three hundred men! But God was with them as they attacked the Midianites, and they won the battle! *(Judges 6:11 thru 8:35)*

Samson and Delilah: God gave Samson the gift of very unusual strength. When he fell in love with a woman named Delilah, she wanted to know the secret of his strength. Even though Samson wasn't supposed to tell anyone, Delilah discovered that Samson's strength came from his hair. So she had Samson's hair cut while he was sleeping. He lost his strength until it grew back again. Although he was able to defeat an entire temple full of Philistines, he died during the battle. *(Judges 13:24 thru 16:30)*

RUTH
A Story of Family Love

AUTHOR:
Unknown

KEY SCRIPTURE:
Where you go I will go, and where you stay I will stay. Your people will be my people and your God my God. *Ruth 1:16*

WHAT THIS BOOK IS ABOUT:
Ruth is about the life of a woman who was faithful to God and family. When Ruth and Naomi's husbands died, Ruth stayed with her mother-in-law to take care of her. When she married a man named Boaz, she became the great-grandmother of David, an ancestor of Jesus, the Messiah.

MAJOR EVENTS:
Ruth stays with Naomi: After their husbands died, Naomi told her two daughters-in-law to return to their home to remarry again. Orpah did as she was told, but Ruth felt a deep love and commitment to her mother-in-law and refused to leave her. *(Ruth 1)*

Ruth marries Boaz: There were very few ways for widows to earn money, so Ruth and Naomi were very poor. Ruth worked in fields, taking what little food was left after it had been harvested. Naomi encouraged Ruth to get to know Boaz, whom she married. Together they had a son. The story of Ruth shows that God has a plan for everyone and watches over us. *(Ruth 2–4)*

PiES OF DooM!

"Looking out for others is for saps!" That's what Otis the Elevated said when Duke Duke challenged him to a pie joust for my hand. But in the end we all learned that looking out for others is true love.

1 Samuel

Learning to Be King

AUTHOR:
Unknown

KEY SCRIPTURE:
You come against me with sword and spear and javelin, but I come against you in the name of the LORD Almighty. *1 Samuel 17:45*

WHAT THIS BOOK IS ABOUT:
The book of 1 Samuel tells about Samuel's life, who was the last judge of Israel. Then it describes the reign of Israel's first king, Saul, and shows how David was prepared to become the next king.

MAJOR EVENTS:
Samuel: Hannah prayed to God for a child and promised to dedicate him to God. God answered her prayer, and Samuel was born. The name Samuel means "asked of God." Samuel grew up and led the people to victory over the evil Philistines. Samuel became a prophet for God. *(1 Samuel 1:1 thru 7:7)*

Rock Slinger;
Rock carving, Tel Halaf, 9th century. B.C.

Saul becomes king: The Israelites wanted a king. So the prophet Samuel anointed Saul as Israel's very first king. Samuel started out as a good king. He defeated his enemies and gave the credit to God. But as time went on, Saul lost faith in God and disobeyed his commands. He was no longer a good king. *(1 Samuel 8–15)*

David and Goliath;
Illustration from a Hebrew manuscript, Northern France, 1280

David and Goliath: A giant Philistine challenged Israel to a fight. But there was no one brave enough to fight the giant! Until a boy named David stepped forward. Trusting God, he used his slingshot and a stone to kill Goliath! *(1 Samuel 17)*

David's rise to king: David had been a shepherd taking care of flocks of sheep. David was chosen by God to be the next king over the Israelites. David had great faith in the Lord. He loved and trusted God with all of his heart. This was the greatest quality a king could have. Saul became jealous of David and tried to have him killed. David responded in patience. He waited for God's timing, instead of his own, to become the next king. *(1 Samuel 18–2 Samuel 10)*

GOD'S GREAT PLANS!

Even though I'm a little guy, God had great plans for me. He used me to defeat the mightiest warrior in the Philistine Army — the Giant Pickle! With God's help, even little guys can do BIG things.

Samuel Anoints David;
Wall painting from the Dura Europus Synagogue, 3rd century

David and Jonathan's friendship: Jonathan was Saul's son. He and David became very close friends. But when Saul became angry and jealous of David, he wanted to have David killed. Jonathan saved his friend's life, even at the cost of betraying his own father. *(1 Samuel 18:1 thru 32:1)*

2 SAMUEL
King David's Reign

AUTHOR:
Unknown

KEY SCRIPTURE:
And David knew that the LORD had established him as king over Israel and had exalted his kingdom for the sake of his people Israel. *2 Samuel 5:12*

WHAT THIS BOOK IS ABOUT:
The book of 2 Samuel is divided into two main ideas that review David's triumphs and troubles. David leads Israel to victory over many nations and shows how much one person can make a difference in the lives of so many.

David also experiences a time of temptation, and he falls into sin. David experiences God's punishment, but also his forgiveness and grace. Second Samuel shows that even those who love God and desire to do his will can fall into temptation and sin. We discover that God's forgiveness is awesome, but the pain of doing wrong can last forever.

MAJOR EVENTS:

David's triumphs: God promised David that he would have a son to reign after him, that his son would build the temple, and that David's family would be established forever. David went on to lead Israel to victory over many enemy nations. *(2 Samuel 1–10)*

David's troubles: While David was king, he committed a terrible sin. He fell in love with a woman named Bathsheba who was married to someone else. Then David sent Bathsheba's husband into a brutal war, knowing he would be killed. David turned away from God. God was willing to forgive David's sins, but David still had to live with pain because of what he had done. *(2 Samuel 11–24)*

1 KINGS
King Solomon's Reign

AUTHOR:
Unknown

KEY SCRIPTURE:
The LORD said to him: "I have heard the prayer and plea you have made before me; I have consecrated this temple, which you have built, by putting my Name there forever. My eyes and my heart will always be there." *1 Kings 9:3*

WHAT THIS BOOK IS ABOUT:
The books of 1 and 2 Kings tell of Israel's history, including the story of King Solomon's rise after the death of David.

God gave King Solomon great wisdom and wealth. Solomon built a beautiful temple for worship and prayer.

Things went well when King Solomon listened to God and used the wisdom he had been given to lead the people. But King Solomon married

King Solomon's Temple;
Wall painting from the Dura Europus Synagogue, 3rd century

women who were not faithful to God. This was something God did not want him to do, and the king began to disobey the Lord.

MAJOR EVENTS:

Solomon becomes king: David's son, Solomon, became the new king. King Solomon did well at first, as he prayed to God for wisdom. God was pleased and made Solomon both the wisest and richest man who had ever lived. Solomon took seven years to build a temple to God. The king became greedy and spent thirteen years building a palace for himself. Solomon also built wonderful cities and powerful armies. God promised Solomon that he would care for his people if he remained faithful like David. Instead, Solomon turned from God and worshiped idols. Soon, the nation turned away from God.

The prophet Elijah: The prophet Elijah told Solomon the people were wrong for disobeying God. God allowed Elijah to call a contest against the prophet of the false god, Baal, to show God's amazing powers!

The Kingdom of Israel Divided

AUTHOR:

Unknown, but possibly Jeremiah

KEY SCRIPTURE:

He did what was right in the eyes of the LORD and walked in all the ways of his father David, not turning aside to the right or to the left. *2 Kings 22:2*

WHAT THIS BOOK IS ABOUT:

The second book of Kings tells how the kingdom of Israel became even further divided. The prophets tried to warn the people about what God would do if they continued to disobey him. But the people refused to listen. The kingdom of Israel was mostly ruled by evil kings, and the prophet Elisha could not help save them.

MAJOR EVENTS:

Elisha's ministry: The people had turned away from God. As Elijah neared the end of his ministry, Elisha tried to restore the people's faith in God. God enabled him to perform miracles to show the people God's amazing power. Elisha tried to show the people the need for trust and faith in God and warned that God's judgment was coming. God allowed him to heal a Shunammite woman's son and Nathan's leprosy. Still, the people would not repent. *(2 Kings 1–17)*

Elisha's Spring;
Near Jericho, where the profit Elisha performed a miracle

1 CHRONICLES

AUTHOR:
Ezra

KEY SCRIPTURE:
Yours, O LORD, is the greatness and the power and the glory and the majesty and the splendor, for everything in heaven and earth is yours. Yours, O LORD, is the kingdom; you are exalted as head over all. *1 Chronicles 29:11*

WHAT THIS BOOK IS ABOUT:
Much of Chronicles repeats what has already been recorded in Samuel and Kings. The main message is to link history to today's time and reassures the people that God is still with them, forever in control, all-powerful, and filled with love for them.

MAJOR EVENTS:
The history of Israel: The books of the Chronicles begin with the listing of history from the creation of Adam through Zerubbabel. It is a reminder that God knows and remembers each one of his children. *(1 Chronicles 1–9)*

King David: The rise of David to the throne is recorded along with his actions that followed. It illustrates David's relationship to God, his devotion to the Lord, and

King David; Illustration from a Hebrew manuscript, Northern France, 1280

Solomon Rock;
Seal bearing on one side the name "Shlomo" (Solomon) in Hebrew letters. On the other side is the figure of a dignified man bearing a scepter, possibly King Solomon

his love and faithfulness. It also points out the promises that David received from God. *(1 Chronicles 10–29)*

2 CHRONICLES

AUTHOR:
Ezra

KEY SCRIPTURE:
If my people, who are called by my name, will humble themselves and pray and seek my face and turn from their wicked ways, then will I hear from heaven and will forgive their sin and will heal their land. *2 Chronicles 7:14*

WHAT THIS BOOK IS ABOUT:
This book focuses on turning the people back to God. The people needed to be reminded how to worship God because God hates sin and he will not tolerate it. So God urged the people to stay away from sin and pointed out that their future depends on their faithfulness to him. Ezra tried to place emphasis on goodness, rather than the failures of good kings. It concludes with the final destruction of the temple and Jerusalem.

Solomon's Temple;
Drawing of the reconstruction of Solomon's temple built in the 9th century. B.C.

MAJOR EVENTS:

King Solomon: Solomon initially ruled with great wisdom that came from God. God used Solomon to build the wonderful temple for the people to worship him. Although Solomon listened to God at first, he became disobedient by marrying women that were unfaithful and pulled him away from God's ways. *(2 Chronicles 1–9)*

Judah's good kings: Ezra showed that Judah had some good kings, including Asa, Jehoshaphat, Uzziah, Hezekiah, and Josiah. *(2 Chronicles 14:1 thru 35:26)*

A nation conquered: Eventually, the Israelites were taken over and the temple was completely ruined. God wanted his people to understand they needed to worship, repent, and change. If that happened, God was willing to forgive them. *(2 Chronicles 36)*

AUTHOR:

Ezra

KEY SCRIPTURE:

With praise and thanksgiving they sang to the LORD: "He is good; his love to Israel endures forever." And all the people gave a great shout of praise to the LORD, because the foundation of the house of the LORD was laid. *Ezra 3:11*

WHAT THIS BOOK IS ABOUT:

Ezra's name means "help." He was a great priest completely dedicated to serving God. The book of Ezra records the fulfillment of God's promise to Israel through Jeremiah to bring them back to their land and rebuild the temple. Ezra taught the people how to worship and serve God.

MAJOR EVENTS:

The return to their homeland: God showed mercy to his people and allowed them to return to their homeland. Upon their return, they rebuilt the temple and the altar, and the people rededicated their lives to God.

Ezra Reads the Law;
Wall painting from the Dura Europus Synagogue, 3rd century

NEHEMIAH

AUTHOR:
Probably Nehemiah. Ezra may have taken part in putting the book together.

KEY SCRIPTURE:
Lord, let your ear be attentive to the prayer of this your servant and to the prayer of your servants who delight in revering your name. *Nehemiah 1:11*

WHAT THIS BOOK IS ABOUT:
Nehemiah was a Hebrew in Persia who asked God to use him in protecting the new city of Jerusalem. God answered his prayer, and the king of Persia allowed him to travel to Jerusalem and build a wall around it. Nehemiah built the wall and was made the governor. Years later, Nehemiah returned to the city and found the walls standing strong, but the people were weak. Then Nehemiah tried to build the principles of the people, a job that was most likely much harder than building a wall.

MAJOR EVENTS:
Building the walls: Nehemiah also wanted to guarantee that the temple would not be destroyed so that worship to God would never be interrupted again. So he wanted to build a wall around the city of Jerusalem. Nehemiah's leadership involved careful planning, courage, and faith in order to get the job done. *(Nehemiah 1–7)*

Nehemiah and Ezra lead the people back to God: After building the walls, Nehemiah had a more difficult task ahead—building up the people of God. With Ezra's help, God enabled them to lead the people to serve God faithfully. *(Nehemiah 8–13)*

The Western Wall
Remains of the west-facing wall that enclosed Herod's temple in Jerusalem. It is the most sacred site in the Jewish world.

Never Be Afraid!

"The battle is not ours. We look to God above. He will guide us safely through and guard us with his love. So do not be afraid. We need not run and hide. For there is nothing we can't face when God is at our side."

AUTHOR:
Unknown

KEY SCRIPTURE:
For if you remain silent at this time, relief and deliverance for the Jews will arise from another place, but you and your father's family will perish. And who knows but that you have come to royal position for such a time as this? *Esther 4:14*

WHAT THIS BOOK IS ABOUT:
The book of Esther is a story about how one person can make a great difference. It tells about a young woman who becomes a queen and risks her life to save the Jewish nation. At the time, no one was allowed to go see the king unless they were invited. Wanting to save her people, Esther showed great courage as she went uninvited to see King Xerxes on two separate occasions. She risked everything by telling the king that his trusted and second-in-command had plotted to destroy her people. The king believed her, and the Jewish nation was saved.

MAJOR EVENTS:
Esther becomes a queen: Queen Vashti refused to obey an order by King Xerxes. She was banished from the kingdom and all the most beautiful women in the kingdom were ordered to appear for him to select from. King Xerxes chose Esther as his new queen. *(Esther 1–2)*

The Jewish people are condemned: Esther's cousin, Mordecai, saved King Xerxes from a plot to kill him. He was made a government official, but he refused to bow to Haman, the king's second-in-command. Haman tricked King Xerxes and persuaded him to create a decree that would destroy Mordecai's people and wipe out the Jewish nation. *(Esther 3–4)*

Esther risks her life: Against the Persian rules, Esther appeared before the king without invitation and asked him to a banquet. She summoned even greater courage and told King Xerxes that his second-in-command had devised a plot to destroy her people. The king was furious. He sentenced Haman to death and appointed Mordecai to be his new second-in-command. *(Esther 5–10)*

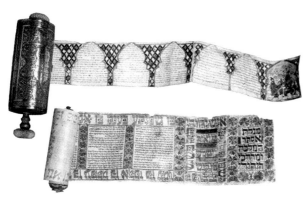

Esther Scroll;
Text read on Purim, a festival commemorating the deliverance of Jews in Persia from massacre

AUTHOR:
Unknown

KEY SCRIPTURE:
Then the LORD said to Satan, "Have you considered my servant Job? There is no one on earth like him; he is blameless and upright, a man who fears God and shuns evil. And he still maintains his integrity, though you incited me against him to ruin him without any reason." *Job 2:3*

WHAT THIS BOOK IS ABOUT:
Job was a very wealthy man who lost everything when his faith was tested. The message of this book illustrates that no one, including Satan, can destroy us, because God has power over all. Everyone wonders why we have to suffer. It can be blamed on punishment for our sins, but God also wants to teach, test, and strengthen us. Remember that God is all we really need, regardless of what happens. Though there is a time and place for sadness, God always deserves our love and our praise.

MAJOR EVENTS:
Job is tested: Job loved and trusted God. He was a wealthy man with a wife and family. Satan came to God and claimed that Job only loved and trusted God because of all of the blessings God gave him. So God allowed Satan to test Job by destroying his family, servants, livestock, home, and health. *(Job 1–2)*

Job suffers: Job suffered terribly due to everything that Satan did to him. His wife and friends told Job to curse God. *(Job 3–37)*

God is in control: Finally, God revealed that he is always in control. Only God has the power to decide who will suffer, how much, in what ways, and why. In the end, Job was satisfied that God—in all his mystery—was enough for him. God rewarded Job and gave him even more riches than he had before. *(Job 38:1–17)*

Job Woodcut;
Germany, 1537

SING TO THE LORD!

I'm very well-known for my clever and entertaining silly songs. Very few people know that some of my favorite songs are Sunday mornin' songs. Did you know that the Psalms are really all songs about God?

King David Playing the Lyre;
Illustration from the Rothschild Miscellany, Northern Italy, 1470

PSALMS

AUTHOR:
David wrote at least seventy-five; Asaph wrote twelve; the sons of Korah wrote ten; Solomon wrote two; Moses wrote one; Heman wrote one; Ethan wrote one; and forty-eight have unknown authors, although it is thought that Ezra contributed to some.

KEY SCRIPTURE:
Create in me a pure heart, O God, and renew a steadfast spirit within me. *Psalm 51:10*

WHAT THIS BOOK IS ABOUT:
The book of Psalms is the longest book in the Bible. It deals with many different topics that include: hymns of praise, thanks, sadness/grief, repentance, trust, hope, and worship. Psalms is a collection of songs, prayers, poems, and praise to and about God.

MAJOR THEMES:
These wonderful expressions of worship come from the heart as an expression of love, adoration, and praise to a holy God. The wide

range of topics covered throughout the book of Psalms is expressed by the writers from their deepest emotions and feelings for God. The Psalms express fear, doubt, praise, worship, and thankfulness; they confess sin and beg forgiveness; they ask for help and express trust; they reflect the bond of love and friendship. Each psalm can be used to guide us in a closer relationship to God our loving Father.

The book of Psalms includes one of the most well-known psalms that Christians turn to for comfort and security:

The LORD is my shepherd, I shall not be in want. He makes me lie down in green pastures, he leads me beside quiet waters, he restores my soul. He guides me in paths of righteousness for his name's sake. Even though I walk through the valley of the shadow of death, I will fear no evil, for you are with me; your rod and your staff, they comfort me. You prepare a table before me in the presence of my enemies. You anoint my head with oil; my cup overflows. Surely goodness and love will follow me all the days of my life, and I will dwell in the house of the LORD forever. *Psalm 23*

PROVERBS

AUTHOR:

First Kings 4:32 tells us that Solomon told 3,000 proverbs and 1,005 songs. Solomon was the writer or collector of most of the Proverbs.

Opening Book of Proverbs;
Illustration from the Rothschild Miscellany, Northern Italy, 1470

KEY SCRIPTURE:

The fear of the LORD is the beginning of wisdom, and knowledge of the Holy One is understanding. *Proverbs 9:10*

WHAT THIS BOOK IS ABOUT:

The book of Proverbs, also called the Book of Wisdom, is a collection of wise sayings. It gives principles for right living based on godly wisdom. These words of wisdom deal with a variety of problems that we experience every day.

MAJOR CATEGORIES:

Wisdom for the young: The first chapters of Proverbs provide wisdom and advice, especially for young people, although it applies to everyone. *(Proverbs 1–9)*

Wisdom for all: The next chapters provide wisdom for daily living. *(Proverbs 10–24)*

Wisdom for leaders: The last chapters show wisdom for leaders or anyone who is looking at being a leader in the future. *(Proverbs 25–31)*

ecclesiastes

AUTHOR:

Solomon

KEY SCRIPTURE:

Now all has been heard; here is the conclusion of the matter: Fear God and keep his commandments, for this is the whole duty of man. *Ecclesiastes 12:13*

WHAT THIS BOOK IS ABOUT:

The book of Ecclesiastes is a teaching about the nature of life. It shows us that worldly pleasures won't fill our lives with a sense of meaning. We learn that life is not always fair. And we discover that our dreams and hopes are ultimately worthless without God.

MAJOR EVENTS:

All worldly things: The first seven chapters of this book describe all the worldly things that Solomon tries to find fulfillment in. He discovered that they are meaningless and have no purpose without God. *(Ecclesiastes 1–7)*

How life should be: The next five chapters describe how life should be lived and come to the conclusion that without God, there is no reason, purpose, or meaning. Even the best of our achievements mean nothing without God in our lives. *(Ecclesiastes 8–12)*

Blessing for the Wedding Couple;
Illustration from the Rothschild Miscellany, Northern Italy, 1470

SONG OF SONGS

AUTHOR:
Solomon

KEY SCRIPTURE:
I am my lover's and my lover is mine; he browses among the lilies. *Song of Songs 6:3*

WHAT THIS BOOK IS ABOUT:
The Song of Songs, also called the Song of Solomon, is a beautiful poem meant to show all the qualities of love between a husband and his wife, as God designed it to be. It shows how a husband and wife should love each other spiritually, emotionally, and physically.

MAJOR EVENTS:
The courtship: Before the wedding, the bride-to-be looked forward to her upcoming marriage. The husband praised his future wife's beauty. *(Song of Songs 2:8 thru 8:4)*

The wedding: The husband once again praised his wife for being so lovely, and the wife expressed her love to her husband. God blessed their union in marriage. *(Song of Songs 1:1 thru 2:7)*

Marriage: As the husband and wife experienced some difficult times, they worked out their problems and remained secure in their love, longing to remain together forever.

ISAIAH

AUTHOR:
Isaiah

KEY SCRIPTURE:
Then I heard the voice of the Lord saying, "Whom shall I send? And who will go for us?" And I said, "Here am I. Send me!" *Isaiah 6:8*

WHAT THIS BOOK IS ABOUT:
Isaiah told the people that they must ask forgiveness from their sins, and he tells of God's judgment and salvation. God won't allow sin to go unpunished, but he is also a God of mercy and compassion.

Isaiah also told about the salvation that the Messiah will bring. He told of how the Messiah would be a light to everyone through him. At the same time, Isaiah also said that the Messiah would suffer for our sins.

Isaiah Scroll;
Part of the Isaiah Scroll, the oldest and longest of the Dead Sea Scrolls, found in Qumran, 100 B.C.

MAJOR EVENTS:

Judgment: Isaiah warned the people to turn away from doing wrong and be obedient to God. The people ignored Isaiah's warnings over and over. *(Isaiah 1–39)*

The coming Messiah: Isaiah brought a message of forgiveness and hope. He prophesied of the coming Messiah as Lord. Isaiah assured the people that God is a God of mercy, grace, and compassion. God provides us all with comfort and hope. God is all-powerful and because of his power, people needn't fear the world around them. God is with us and he will help us. Isaiah 41:10 says: "So do not fear, for I am with you; do not be dismayed, for I am your God. I will strengthen you and help you; I will uphold you with my righteous right hand." Isaiah also prophesied that the Messiah would suffer and forgive everyone who has faith in him. *(Isaiah 40–66)*

AUTHOR:

Jeremiah

KEY SCRIPTURE:

"For I know the plans I have for you," declares the LORD, "plans to prosper you and not to harm you, plans to give you hope and a future. *Jeremiah 29:11*

Assyrian War Chariot;
Relief from Sanaherib's palace in Ninveh, 700 B.C.

WHAT THIS BOOK IS ABOUT:

Jeremiah prophesied about Israel and Judah, warning the people to be obedient to God, to repent of their sins and turn from their evil ways. But the people did not listen.

MAJOR EVENTS:

Jeremiah proclaims God's judgment: Jeremiah proclaimed God's messages to the people and warned them to turn from sin and idolatry. The people would not listen. Jeremiah warned the people about God's judgment, but they still wouldn't listen. Jeremiah was willing to live as a poor man, he was rejected by family, friends, neighbors, and false priests, and he even got thrown into jail in order to proclaim God's messages. *(Jeremiah 1–38)*

The fall of Jerusalem: God looked upon Jeremiah favorably because of Jeremiah's great faith and commitment. Then many of Jeremiah's prophecies took place, including the fall of Jerusalem, because the people refused to turn away from sin. Even though God showed a harsh judgment, he does promise that he will ultimately restore the land. *(Jeremiah 40–52)*

LamenTaTions

AUTHOR:

Jeremiah

KEY SCRIPTURE:

Because of the LORD's great love we are not consumed, for his compassions never fail. They are new every morning; great is your faithfulness. *Lamentations 3:22–23*

WHAT THIS BOOK IS ABOUT:

The word Lamentation means "to express suffering." As a result of Judah's disobedience, God allowed the Babylonians to destroy the city of Jerusalem. This book is divided into five different poems that express Jeremiah's deep sorrow and pain due to the fall of Jerusalem.

MAJOR EVENTS:

Jeremiah's sorrow: This poem describes Jeremiah's pain due to the fall of Jerusalem. *(Lamentations 1)*

Hope FOR THE Journey!

Remember, wherever you go and whatever you do, God has great plans and will take care of you! I've done a lot of traveling and I can tell you that he's everywhere... even Pugsleyville!

Ezekiel's Prophecy;
The destruction and restoration of natural life. Wall painting from Dura Europos, 245 A.D.

God's anger: This poem describes God's anger at the people due to their refusal to turn away from sin and idolatry. *(Lamentations 2)*

Jeremiah's hope: This poem describes Jeremiah's reflection on God's compassion and love that provides hope for the future. *(Lamentations 3)*

God's punishment: This poem describes the pain of the people and the destruction of the city because of their refusal to turn from sin. *(Lamentations 4)*

Jeremiah pleas for forgiveness: This poem describes how Jeremiah turned to God, asking for mercy, forgiveness, and an end to the suffering. *(Lamentations 5)*

ezekiel

AUTHOR:
Ezekiel

KEY SCRIPTURE:
And the name of the city from that time on will be: The LORD is There. *Ezekiel 48:35*

WHAT THIS BOOK IS ABOUT:
The prophet Ezekiel lived in Babylon during the time when the Jewish people were cast out. This book records his ministry, which predicts the destruction of Jerusalem due to God's judgment because the people would not turn away from sin. Ezekiel encouraged the people to turn away from doing wrong and evil things, but the people refused to listen.

MAJOR EVENTS:

Ezekiel warns the people: The people blamed God for the destruction of the city and claimed that he could do nothing to save them. But the destruction was God's will and punishment upon the people because they refused to turn away from sin. *(Ezekiel 1–32)*

Ezekiel provides hope: After the destruction of Jerusalem, Ezekiel proclaimed messages of good news to the people. His message was that God would restore the city and all of God's promises would be fulfilled. *(Ezekiel 33–48)*

AUTHOR:

Daniel

KEY SCRIPTURE:

For he is the living God and he endures forever; his kingdom will not be destroyed, his dominion will never end. *Daniel 6:26*

WHAT THIS BOOK IS ABOUT:

Daniel was obediently faithful to God, but he also served in the royal court of King Nebuchadnezzar and King Darius. This book reviews Daniel's amazing stories of faith, prophecies, and visions.

MAJOR EVENTS:

Shadrach, Meshach, and Abednego's faith: Shadrach, Meshach, and Abednego refused to bow down to the image of King Nebuchadnezzar, so they were sentenced to a fiery death. They never lost faith, and God saved their lives. *(Daniel 3)*

Daniel's faith: Daniel remained faithful to God and continued to pray to him, despite the schemes and warnings by King Darius that no one should pray to anyone other than him. King Darius sentenced Daniel to death, this time in a den of lions. God closed the

STAND UP!

When everybody tells you that you gotta be cool, remember what you learned in church and Sunday school. Just check it out. The Bible tells us what it's all about. Stand up for what you believe in. God will stand with you!

Don't cry, Daniel.
Fear not, Daniel.
Don't you know you're
not alone? There is
one who is watching
you. He listens when
you pray. And though
it seems this time you
won't get through,
God will have a way!

mouths of the lions, and Daniel life was saved. Wheb King Darius saw how God saved Daniel, he called for all people to worship Daniel's God. *(Daniel 1–6)*

Daniel's visions: God provided Daniel with visions to let the people know that God is in control of the future and he wants us to faithfully obey and worship him. *(Daniel 7:1–13)*

HOSEA

AUTHOR:
Hosea

KEY SCRIPTURE:
Who is wise? He will realize these things. Who is discerning? He will understand them. The ways of the LORD are right; the righteous walk in them, but the rebellious stumble in them. *Hosea 14:9*

WHAT THIS BOOK IS ABOUT:
The book of Hosea describes the relationship between God and the people of Israel. God asked Hosea to marry a woman who did not remain faithful to him.

Despite his wife being unfaithful, Hosea forgave her, took her back in, and loved her. This is similar to the people of Israel who were made to suffer God's punishment because of their behavior, yet God ultimately showed them love and compassion.

MAJOR EVENTS:
Hosea marries: The life of Hosea is a symbolic reminder of God's unconditional love. Hosea fell in love with, married, and was devoted to his wife Gomer, who left him repeatedly. *(Hosea 1–3)*

God's people are disobedient: Hosea's wife turned away from Hosea despite how much he loved her. God's people have turned their backs on him since the beginning of time. Hosea's message tells us also about the coming of the Messiah (Jesus), and his prophecies are often quoted in the New Testament. *(Hosea 4–14)*

Daniel and the Lions;
Possibly the base stone of a synagogue ark, Ein Nashut, Golan.

JOEL

AUTHOR:
Joel

KEY SCRIPTURE:
Return to the LORD your God, for he is gracious and compassionate, slow to anger and abounding in love. *Joel 2:13*

WHAT THIS BOOK IS ABOUT:
The book of Joel describes a swarm of locusts that caused disaster to Israel. Joel called the nation of Judah to a day of repentance so God would be merciful and forgive them.

MAJOR EVENTS:
The plague of locusts: Joel described a terrible swarm of locusts that descended upon Israel and destroyed their crops. Joel explained that this is an example of God's coming judgment. *(Joel 1:1 thru 2:27)*

The "Day of the Lord": Joel described God's judgment and the need to seek God's forgiveness. Without repentance, God's judgment will be harsh and certain. *(Joel 2:28 thru 3:21)*

amos

AUTHOR:
Amos

KEY SCRIPTURE:
But let justice roll on like a river, righteousness like a never-failing stream! *Amos 5:24*

WHAT THIS BOOK IS ABOUT:
God gave Amos a vision of what was to come for the nation of Israel. He warned the people that they should turn from their sin—materialism, and acting immoral. He urged the people to repent before the judgment of God was upon them. Amos's plea to the people was to "Seek God and live."

MAJOR EVENTS:
Judgment: Amos saw how Israel was becoming dishonest and neglecting God's law. God judged them because of their greed, idolatry, materialism, and refusal to help the poor. Amos courageously told the people to repent; God's judgment was near and God promised to help them in the future. *(Amos 1–9)*

Mountains of Edom;
Western Jordan

OBADIAH

AUTHOR:
Obadiah

KEY SCRIPTURE:
The day of the Lord is near for all nations. As you have done, it will be done to you; your deeds will return upon your own head. *Obadiah 1:15*

WHAT THIS BOOK IS ABOUT:
Obadiah, the shortest book in the Old Testament, condemns Edom for their sins against God and Israel. These people are the descendants of Esau. Obadiah warns them that they cannot escape God's judgment.

MAJOR EVENT:
Edom is destroyed: Obadiah's message is certain. The kingdom of Edom will be destroyed because the people refused to obey God.

JONAH

AUTHOR:
Jonah

KEY SCRIPTURE:
In my distress I called to the LORD, and he answered me. From the depths of the grave I called for help, and you listened to my cry. *Jonah 2:2*

WHAT THIS BOOK IS ABOUT:
God asks the prophet Jonah to warn the city of Nineveh to stop doing wrong, repent, and obey his commands. Jonah does not want to preach this message to the Ninevites, so he runs away in the opposite direction. As a result, Jonah is swallowed up by a big fish and then spit back out three days later. Then Jonah finally delivers God's message, but does not understand God's mercy and compassion for the people there.

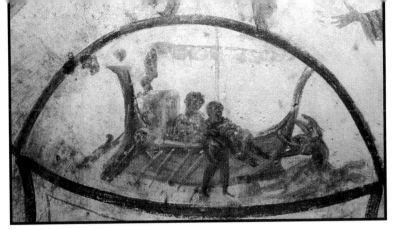

Jonah Thrown Overboard;
Roman catacomb wall painting, 2-3rd century

MAJOR EVENTS:

Jonah disobeys: God requested that Jonah deliver a message to the Ninevites that they turn away from their wicked ways to avoid his judgment. Jonah refused to deliver God's message and wound up in the belly of a big fish where he prayed to God for mercy. Three days later, the fish spit him back out and Jonah was given a second chance to deliver the message. *(Jonah 1–2)*

Jonah delivers God's message: Jonah went to Nineveh and delivered God's message. He told the people to stop doing wrong and repent of their evil ways. The people listened to the message and asked for God's mercy. Jonah was displeased that the people were not punished.

AUTHOR:

Micah

KEY SCRIPTURE:

He has shown you, O man, what is good. And what does the LORD require of you? To act justly and to love mercy and to walk humbly with your God. *Micah 6:8*

WHAT THIS BOOK IS ABOUT:

Micah has a message of God's judgment and hope. He tells Israel to end their disobedience toward God and to stop worshiping idols. Micah also tells the people that God will help and forgive those who ask him and turn away from sin.

message From The Lord!

God's the God of mercy. God's the God of love. Right now he's gonna lend a helping hand from up above. If you say you're sorry for all the stuff you do, you know that he'll be ready with a second chance for you.

Habakkuk Comentary;
Dead Sea Scrolls. An early type of Jewish biblical commentary
explaining the philosophy of the 7th-century B.C. prophet Habakkuk

MAJOR EVENT:

Micah's warning: Micah condemned the rulers and leaders of Israel who misled the people. He warned that Jerusalem would be destroyed. Micah also told the people that God wants justice, obedience, and loyalty.

AUTHOR:

Nahum

KEY SCRIPTURE:

The LORD is good, a refuge in times of trouble. He cares for those who trust in him. *Nahum 1:7*

WHAT THIS BOOK IS ABOUT:

The book of Nahum was written 150 years after Jonah was sent to Nineveh with God's message that the people were to repent and turn from their evil ways. The Ninevites had turned their backs on God and overpowered the northern kingdom of Israel and brought them into captivity. Nahum proclaimed a message of doom for Nineveh.

AUTHOR:

Habakkuk

KEY SCRIPTURE:

LORD, I have heard of your fame; I stand in awe of your deeds, O LORD. Renew them in our day, in our time make them known; in wrath remember mercy. *Habakkuk 3:2*

WHAT THIS BOOK IS ABOUT:

Habakkuk complained about the bad things in the world and did not understand why God allowed his people to suffer at the hands of their enemies. God's answer was that the people must continue to trust in his mercy and compassion, no matter what happens. Although the wicked appear to be doing well, their success is only temporary. God will never leave those who are faithful and follow him.

AUTHOR:

Zephaniah

KEY SCRIPTURE:

Seek the LORD, all you humble of the land, you who do what he commands. Seek righteousness, seek humility; perhaps you will be sheltered on the day of the LORD's anger. *Zephaniah 2:3*

WHAT THIS BOOK IS ABOUT:

Zephaniah gives the people a message of judgment and encouragement. He promises that God is supreme. He explains that God will punish the wicked and show mercy to the faithful. He blesses those who are truly sorry, who ask for his forgiveness and put their trust in him.

AUTHOR:

Haggai

KEY SCRIPTURE:

Now this is what the LORD Almighty says: "Give careful thought to your ways. You have planted much, but have harvested little. You eat, but never have enough. You drink, but never have your fill. You put on clothes, but are not warm. You earn wages, only to put them in a purse with holes in it." *Haggai 1:5–6*

WHAT THIS BOOK IS ABOUT:

Haggai wanted to challenge the people, their decisions, and their faithfulness. Haggai tried to motivate the people and encouraged them to place God as a priority in their lives. Haggai called the people to glorify God by building the temple that Solomon built, which had been destroyed many years before. He encouraged them to turn away from evil and trust in God, because God would provide for their needs.

Tomb of Zechariah;
Rock-hewn structure in the Kidron Valley, east of the Temple Mount, built in the 1st-century B.C.

ZECHARIAH  MALACHI

AUTHOR:
Zechariah

AUTHOR:
Malachi

KEY SCRIPTURE:
Therefore tell the people: This is what the LORD Almighty says: "Return to me," declares the LORD Almighty, "and I will return to you," says the LORD Almighty. *Zechariah 1:3*

KEY SCRIPTURE:
"They will be mine," says the LORD Almighty, "in the day when I make up my treasured possession. I will spare them, just as in compassion a man spares his son who serves him. And you will again see the distinction between the righteous and the wicked, between those who serve God and those who do not." *Malachi 3:17–18*

WHAT THIS BOOK IS ABOUT:
Like Haggai, Zechariah encouraged the people to rebuild the temple too. In addition to this, Zechariah told of visions he had about the coming of the Messiah (Jesus), who would rescue the people and reign over the earth. There are many prophecies in this book that were fulfilled in the life of Jesus Christ.

WHAT THIS BOOK IS ABOUT:
Malachi's message was for God's people who had turned away from him. The people were waiting for the coming Messiah (Jesus) and again acted disobediently. Even the priests weren't honoring God's promises. They were not worshiping as they should, nor were they giving what God had commanded.

Tomb of Zechariah;
Engraving by the British artist, Traveler Roberts, from 1830-1840

THe new TesTamenT

Mary and Jesus;
Mosaic from Hagia Sophia, Istambul, 12th century

AUTHOR:
Matthew

KEY SCRIPTURE:
Therefore go and make disciples of all nations, baptizing them in the name of the Father and of the Son and of the Holy Spirit, and teaching them to obey everything I have commanded you. And surely I am with you always, to the very end of the age. *Matthew 28:19–20*

WHAT THIS BOOK IS ABOUT:
The book of Matthew tells about the birth, ministry, death, and resurrection of Jesus Christ. Matthew is one of Jesus' twelve disciples who attempts to prove to the Jews that Jesus is the promised Messiah.

MAJOR EVENTS:
The birth of Jesus: The people were waiting for the promised Messiah to help them, like the prophets had promised. An angel told Joseph in a dream that Jesus was going to be born, and that he and Mary would be his parents. Jesus was born in a manger. *(Matthew 1–2)*

John the Baptist: John the Baptist prepared the way for Jesus by telling the people that Jesus was the Messiah the prophets told them about. John said they should ask God's forgiveness for their sins, and pledge their faithfulness to God through baptism. John baptized Jesus. *(Matthew 3)*

Mt. of Beatitudes;
Overlooking the Sea of Galilee, built on the site where Jesus proclaimed the Beatitudes
to the crowd of listeners

Jesus is tempted by Satan: Jesus fasted for fourty days in the desert. While he was there, Satan tempted him three times but Jesus never sinned. *(Matthew 4:1–11)*

The ministry of Jesus: Jesus called twelve disciples to follow him. He taught the people about God's love, healed the sick, performed miracles, offered forgiveness for sins, and showed the way to heaven.

Jesus taught: Jesus delivered the Sermon on the Mount to tell people how to live.

The Lord's Prayer: Jesus went on to teach the people many things about God. One of those teachings was how to pray. From that, we received THE LORD'S PRAYER:

"This, then, is how you should pray: 'Our Father in heaven, hallowed be your name, your kingdom come, your will be done, on earth as it is in heaven. Give us today our daily bread. Forgive us our debts, as we also have forgiven our debtors. And lead us not into temptation, but deliver us from the evil one.'" *(Matthew 6:5–15)*

Jesus performs miracles: Jesus performed many miracles to demonstrate the power of God.

The miracles of Jesus:

Here is a list of the miracles Jesus performed, as recorded in each of the Gospels:

He heals a leper. (*Matthew 8:1–4; Mark 1:40–42; Luke 5:12–13*)

Heals a centurion's servant. (*Matthew 8:5–13; Luke 7:1–10*)

He heals Peter's mother-in-law. (*Matthew 8:14–15; Mark 1:30–31; Luke 4:38–39*)

He calms a storm. (*Matthew 8:23–27; Mark 4:35–41; Luke 8:22–25*)

Casts the devil out of two men. (*Matthew 8:28–34; Mark 5:1–15; Luke 8:27–35*)

He heals a paralyzed man. (*Matthew 9:1–8; Mark 2:1–12; Luke 5:18–25*)

Raises Jairus's daughter. (*Matthew 9:18–26; Mark 5:22–24; Luke 8:41–42*)

Heals a woman's bleeding. (*Matthew 9:20–22; Mark 5:25–29; Luke 8:43–48*)

Jesus heals a blind man and a mute. (*Matthew 9:27–31*)

Casts out a demon. (*Matthew 9:32–33*)

Heals a man's hand. (*Matthew 12:9–13; Mark 3:1–5; Luke 6:6–10*)

Heals a demon-possessed man. (*Matthew 12:22–37; Luke 11:14*)

He feeds a hungry crowd of five thousand with five small loaves of bread and two fish. (*Matthew 14:15–21; Mark 6:35–44; Luke 9:12–17; John 6:5–13*)

He walks on water. (*Matthew 14:22–33; Mark 6:48–51; John 6:19–21*)

Heals a woman's daughter. (*Matthew 15:21–28; Mark 7:24–30*)

He feeds over four thousand people. (*Matthew 15:32–39; Mark 8:1–9*)

The transfiguration. (*Matthew 17:1–8*)

Heals a child. (*Matthew 17:14–21; Mark 9:17–29; Luke 9:38–43*)

He predicts a coin would be in a fish's mouth. (*Matthew 17:24–27*)

He commands a fig tree to die. (*Matthew 21:18–22; Mark 11:12–26*)

Casts out a demon. (*Mark 1:23–26; Luke 4:33–35*)

Heals a man who couldn't hear or speak. (*Mark 7:31–37*)

Heals a blind man. (*Mark 8:22–26*)

He causes a large catch of fish. (*Luke 5:1–11*)

He heals a man with leprosy. (*Luke 5:1–15*)

Raises a woman's son. (*Luke 7:11–35*)

Raises Lazarus. (*Luke 11:1–46*)

Heals a man in a Pharisee's house. (*Luke 14:1–6*)

Heals ten lepers. (*Luke 17:11–19*)

Heals Malchus's ear. (*Luke 22:49–51*)

He turns water into wine. (*John 2:1–11*)

He heals a man's son in Galilee. (*John 4:43–54*)

Heals a man born blind. (*John 9:1–17*)

The resurrection. (*John 21:1–14*)

The Last Supper;
Drawing from Codex 2, a 15th-century illuminated manuscript from
the Monastery of Iveron on Mt. Athos

Crataegus Thorn;
Believed to be the thorn from which Jesus' crown was made

The death of Jesus: Jesus celebrated the Passover meal with his disciples, which is known as the Last Supper. Judas, one of his disciples, betrayed Jesus. Jesus was put on trial and sentenced to death, even though he did nothing wrong. Jesus was beaten and made to carry his own cross to Golgotha where he was crucified and died. Jesus died to take away the sins of everyone who believes in him. *(Matthew 26:14 thru 27:56)*

Jesus is risen: Jesus' body was placed in a tomb, and a large stone was rolled in front of the entrance, and it was guarded by a Roman soldier. Several women went to visit the tomb, but the stone had been rolled away. Jesus appeared to them and told them to tell the others that he was risen from the death. Jesus is alive! *(Matthew 27:57 thru 28:20)*

The Galilee Boat;
Recently excavated from the
mud at the bottom of the Sea of
Galilee, dating from the 1st century

AUTHOR:

Mark

KEY SCRIPTURE:

"Let the little children come to me, and do not hinder them, for the kingdom of God belongs to such as these. I tell you the truth, anyone who will not receive the kingdom of God like a little child will never enter it." And he took the children in his arms, put his hands on them and blessed them. *Mark 10:14–16*

WHAT THIS BOOK IS ABOUT:

Mark, a relative of Barnabas, traveled with Paul. The book of Mark tells of Jesus' teachings, miracles, and the problems he had with the religious leaders. Mark tells how Jesus was the Lord and the Savior of the world.

MAJOR EVENTS:

Jesus' ministry: The Gospel of Mark explains more about Jesus' actions and what he did to prove that he is God's Son. Jesus did a lot to teach and heal others. This book follows Jesus' journey through Galilee and other areas and reviews how he touched many lives. *(Mark 1–13)*

Jesus chooses the twelve disciples: Jesus chose twelve disciples to be with him throughout his ministry. They came from many different experiences and backgrounds. Jesus chose them because they were willing to obey and follow him in spreading God's Word. After Jesus died, they were filled with the Holy Spirit and empowered to carry on his ministry. The disciples were: Simon Peter, James, John, Andrew, Philip, Bartholomew, Matthew, Thomas, James, Thaddeus, Simon the Zealot, and Judas Iscariot.

Prison of Christ;
Where Jesus spent the night after being arrested at Gethsemane

Via Dolorosa Ecco Homo;
Second station along the Via Dolorosa, where Pilate presented Christ to the crowd by saying "Ecce Homo" (behold the man)

Jesus' last week:

Jesus tried to prepare his disciples that he would die, but they did not understand. Finally, after a three-year ministry, it came time to go to Jerusalem for the Passover. This was the start of Jesus' last week:

Sunday: Jesus entered Jerusalem from the Mount of Olives, riding on a donkey. The crowds welcomed him as the promised Messiah. *(Mark 11:1–10)*

Monday: Jesus threw the dishonest merchants out of the temple, God's house of prayer. *(Mark 11:15–18)*

Tuesday: Jesus taught in the temple. *(Mark 12:1–44)*

Wednesday: Judas agreed to betray Jesus. *(Mark 14:10–11)*

Thursday: Jesus and his twelve disciples had the Last Supper together. Later that night, Jesus prayed in the Garden of Gethsemane, where he was betrayed by Judas and arrested. *(Mark 14:12–25)*

Friday: Jesus was tried before Annas, Caiaphas, and the Jewish Sanhedrin. Jesus was taken before Pilate and sentenced to death. Jesus was beaten, was hung on a cross, died, and was buried. *(Mark 14:43 thru 15:40)*

Sunday: Jesus rose from the dead! (Luke 24)

Church of St. Peter Gallicantu;
Location where Peter denied Christ three times before the crow of the rooster.

Jesus appears to others: Mary Magdalene, Mary the mother of James, and Salome brought spices to care for Jesus' body. When they arrived at the tomb, they saw the stone rolled away. An angel told them that Jesus had risen from death and was alive! They ran to tell the others, and Jesus appeared to Mary Magdalene. Later, Jesus also appeared to all of his disciples, including Thomas, who doubted that he had really risen. *(Mark 15:42 thru 16:20)*

AUTHOR:

Luke

KEY SCRIPTURE:

For unto you is born this day in the city of David a Saviour, which is Christ the lord. And this shall be a sign unto you; Ye shall find the babe

Golgotha;
The skull-shaped rock near the Garden Tomb that was the place of Jesus' crucifixion

Announciation;
Drawing from Codex 2, a 15th-century
illuminated manuscript from the Monastery
of Iveron on Mt. Athos

wrapped in swaddling clothes, lying in a manger. And suddenly there was with the angel a multitude of heavenly host praising God, and saying, Glory to God in the highest, and on earth peace, good will toward men. *Luke 2:11–14 (KJV)*

WHAT THIS BOOK IS ABOUT:

Luke traveled with Paul, and he also wrote the book of Acts. In Luke, he tells about the birth, life, death, and resurrection of Jesus Christ. Luke emphasizes that Jesus is not only the Son of God, but also the Son of Man.

Mary and Joseph traveled to Bethlehem because Caesar Augustus was conducting a census of all the people. A census means he was counting everybody. That sure would be a lot of counting.

MAJOR EVENTS:

An angel appears to Mary: An angel appeared to Mary to tell her that she would be the mother of Jesus. Mary visited her relative Elizabeth, who also was going to have a baby. Elizabeth's baby was known as John the Baptist. *(Luke 1:26–80)*

Jesus' birth and childhood: Mary and Joseph had to travel to Bethlehem to register for a census. In Bethlehem, baby Jesus was born in a manger. An angel announced the birth to the shepherds. At age twelve, Jesus traveled to the temple with his parents for the Feast of the Passover and spent time with the religious leaders in the temple courts. *(Luke 2:1–51)*

The Star of Bethleche;
The silver star under the altar in the Basilica of the Nativity marks the spot where it is believed Jesus was born

The ministry of Jesus: Jesus' ministry shows his love, compassion, and forgiveness through his stories and healings. Jesus offers forgiveness and salvation that is available to everyone who believes

Love Your Neighbor!

I have a shoe and he has pot, but when we look deeper there's more that we've got. God made us special and now I can see, if you're special to him then you're special to me.

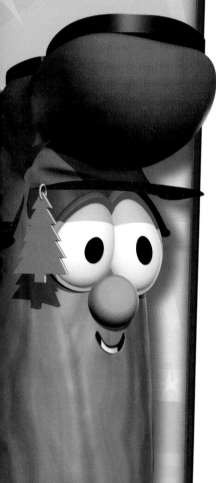

Almond Blossoms;
Spring in Galilee, a similar view to what Jesus would have seen as he taught

in him. Jesus tells us to treat others the way we want to be treated. *(Luke 4:14 thru 21:38)*

Jesus taught the people: Jesus said the most important commandment is to "'Love the Lord your God with all your heart and with all your soul and with all your strength and with all your mind,' and, 'Love your neighbor as yourself.'" *(Luke 10:27)*

Jesus taught by telling stories called parables: Jesus also taught in parables. A parable is a story that teaches a lesson. This is a parable of the Good Samaritan:

Jesus said: "A man was going down from Jerusalem to Jericho, when he fell into the hands of robbers. They stripped him of his clothes, beat him and went away, leaving him half dead. A priest happened to be going down the same road, and when he saw the man, he passed by on the other side. So too, a Levite, when he came to the place and saw him, passed by on the other side. But a Samaritan, as he traveled, came where the man was; and when he saw him, he took pity on him. He went to him and bandaged his wounds, pouring on oil and wine. Then he put the man on his own donkey, took him to an inn and took care of him. The next day he took out two silver coins and gave them to the innkeeper. 'Look after him,' he said, 'and when I return, I will reimburse you for any extra expense you may have.'

"Which of these three do you think was a neighbor to the man who fell into the hands of robbers?"

The expert in the law replied, "The one who had mercy on him." Jesus told him, "Go and do likewise." *(Luke 10:30–37)*

Jesus told parables:

Jesus told parables to teach the people lessons they needed to learn.

He taught parables about the kingdom of God:

The Soils *(Matthew 13:3-8; Mark 4:4–8; Luke 8:5–8)*

The Weeds *(Matthew 13:24–30)*

The Mustard Seed *(Matthew 13:31–32; Mark 4:30–32; Luke 13:18–19)*

The Yeast *(Matthew 13:33; Luke 13:20–21)*

The Treasure *(Matthew 13:44)*

The Pearl *(Matthew 13:45–46)*

The Fishing Net *(Matthew 13:47–50)*

The Growing Wheat *(Mark 4:26–29)*

He taught parables about serving and obedience:

The Workers in the Harvest *(Matthew 20:1–16)*

The Loaned Money *(Matthew 25:14–30)*

The Nobleman's Servants *(Luke 19:11–27)*

The Servant's role *(Luke 17:7–10)*

He taught parables about prayer:

The Friend at Midnight *(Luke 11:5–8)*

The Unjust Judge *(Luke 18:1–8)*

He taught parables about neighbors:

The Good Samaritan *(Luke 10:30–37)*

He taught parables about humility:

The Wedding Feast *(Luke 14:7–11)*

The Proud Pharisee and the Corrupt Tax Collector *(Luke 18:9–14)*

He taught parables about wealth:

The Rich Fool *(Luke 12:16–21)*

The Great Feast *(Luke 14:16–24)*

The Shrewd Manager *(Luke 16:1–9)*

He taught parables about love:

The Lost Sheep *(Matthew 18:12–14; Luke 15:3–7)*

The Lost Coin *(Luke 15:8–10)*

The Lost Son *(Luke 15:11–32)*

He taught parables about thankfulness:

The forgiven debts *(Luke 7:41–43)*

He taught parables about his return.

The Ten Virgins *(Matthew 25:1–13)*

The Wise and Faithful Servants *(Matthew 24:45–51; Luke 12:42–48)*

The Traveling Owner of the House *(Mark 13:34–37)*

He taught parables about God's values.

The Two Sons *(Matthew 21:28–32)*

The Wicked Tenants *(Matthew 21:33–34; Mark 12:1–9; Luke 20:9–16)*

The Unproductive Fig Tree *(Luke 13:6–9)*

The Marriage Feast *(Matthew 22:1–14)*

The Unforgiving Servant *(Matthew 18:23–35)*

FRIENDS FOREVER!

Bob and I have been best friends for years! I don't know where I'd be without him. Did you know that John was one of Jesus' best friends? I wonder how many videos they did together?

The death of Jesus: Jesus' enemies wanted his death on a cross. Jesus was betrayed, arrested, tried, and crucified. *(Luke 22:1 thru 23:49)*

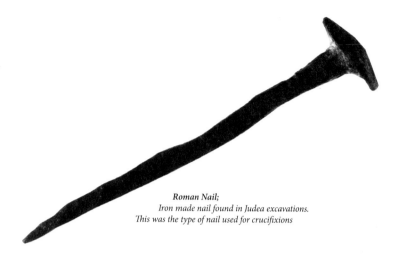

Roman Nail;
Iron made nail found in Judea excavations.
This was the type of nail used for crucifixions

Jesus is risen: Jesus rose from the dead and went to heaven. His resurrection proves that we can trust Jesus as our Savior. We can go to heaven through faith in Jesus. *(Luke 23:49 thru 24:53)*

AUTHOR:
John

KEY SCRIPTURE:
For God so loved the world that he gave his one and only Son, that whoever believes in him shall not perish but have eternal life. *John 3:16*

WHAT THIS BOOK IS ABOUT:
John closes his book (20:31) by telling us: *But these are written that you may believe that Jesus is the Christ, the Son of God, and that by believing you may have life in his name.* John was called the disciple whom Jesus loved. He was one of the twelve disciples of Jesus. John wanted to help everyone understand that Jesus is Son of God.

MAJOR EVENTS:
The preparation for Jesus: The book of John starts at the very beginning of time: *In the beginning was the Word, and the Word was with God, and the Word was God. He was with God in the beginning.*

Transfiguration;
Drawing from an 11th-century gospel dictionary from the Monastery of Iveron on Mt. Athos

(John 1:1–2) John proved that Jesus was indeed the Son of God, the waited-for Messiah, and our Savior. *(Luke 1:1 thru 2:11)*

Teachings about Jesus: Jesus reveals who he is through the various titles he gives himself throughout his teachings. "I am the bread of life." *(John 6:35)* "I am the light of the world." *(John 8:12 and 9:5)* "I am the gate." *(John 10:7)* "I am the good shepherd." *(John 10:11, 14)* "I am the resurrection and the life." *(John 11:25)* "I am the way and the truth and the life." *(John 14:6)* "I am the true vine." *(John 15:1)*

The Holy Spirit: Jesus taught that those who believe in Jesus would receive the Holy Spirit, teach, convict, and guide in the truth. *(John 14:25–26, 16:5–16)*

The death and resurrection of Jesus: Jesus willingly died on the cross in our place to forgive our sins. He paid our debt in full so that whoever puts their faith and trust in him will be saved. *(John 18–21)*

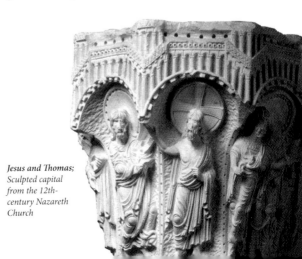

Jesus and Thomas;
Sculpted capital from the 12th-century Nazareth Church

Peter Raises Tabitha from the Dead;
Sculpted capital from the 12th-century Nazareth Church

AUTHOR:
Luke, who traveled with Paul, and also wrote the Gospel of Luke

KEY SCRIPTURE:
Believe in the Lord Jesus, and you will be saved—you and your household. *Acts 16:31*

WHAT THIS BOOK IS ABOUT:
The book of Acts focuses on the apostles and how they were witnesses for Christ after he rose from the dead and on the growth of the church.

MAJOR EVENTS:
The start of a new church: After the resurrection of Jesus, the disciples carried on his ministry to start new churches. A new disciple, Matthias, was appointed to replace Judas, who had betrayed Jesus. The Holy Spirit came upon those who believed in Jesus on the day of Pentecost. The Holy Spirit allowed believers to speak in different languages, allowing everyone in the crowd to hear God's message. *(Acts 1–8)*

Saul's conversion: Saul began his adult life as a Roman soldier who hated Christ followers. One day, on his way to Damascus, a light from heaven flashed around him. Jesus asked Saul why he was persecuting and hurting him and his people. When Saul got up, he was blind. Jesus told him to go into the city where a man named Ananias placed his hands on him and he could see again. Saul was baptized and spent time with Jesus' disciples to learn more about him. God changed Saul's name to Paul. *(Acts 9:1–22)*

Peter's miraculous escape: King Herod had arrested some people who belonged to the church and planned to kill them. Peter was one of them. The church prayed to God for their release. The night before he was to be brought before trial, Peter was sleeping between two guards, bound by chains. An angel of the Lord appeared and told Peter to get up. The chains fell off of him and the others. They passed the guards, and the gates miraculously opened for them. *(Acts 12:1–18)*

The ministry of Paul: After his conversion, Paul was completely changed as the Holy Spirit worked through him to proclaim the Word of

Via Apia;
The ancient paved road leading to Rome, built in 194 B.C. Paul was lead to prison on this road in 56 A.D.

God to those who had never heard about Jesus. Paul went on three major missionary tours. *(Acts 13–28)*

Paul and Silas in prison: As Paul and Silas were trying to help a slave girl, they were seized by the Roman soldiers, beaten, and thrown into prison. Even in jail, Paul and Silas sang hymns to God. At midnight there was a terrible earthquake. It caused the prison doors to open and the prisoner's chains to come loose. Paul and Silas told the jailer about Jesus. The jailer and all of his family believe in Jesus and were baptized. *(Acts 16)*

Prison of Paul;
Ruins of the ancient church in Philippi, built on the site believed to have been the prison where Paul was detained.

Paul's shipwreck: Paul was in prison for preaching about Jesus. He and other prisoners were put on board a ship, but as they traveled, the winds became dangerous.

Paul told them that an angel had appeared to him and said they should take courage. God would spare everyone with him, although their boat would be shattered. Everything happened as the angel said that it would. The ship was destroyed, but all of the people made it safely to shore.

Statue of Paul;
Located at the entrance to the Basilica of S. Paolo Fuori de Mura. Place of
Paul's burial on the way to Ostia, near Rome.

AUTHOR:

Paul

KEY SCRIPTURE:

For the wages of sin is death, but the gift of God is eternal life in Christ Jesus our Lord. *Romans 6:23*

WHAT THIS BOOK IS ABOUT:

Paul wrote a letter to the Christians in Rome, excited about his ministry and ability to spread the good news of Jesus Christ. Paul talks about the need to practice obedience, practice faith, and use the gifts God has given us. Although Paul told the people to stop doing bad things, he also says we are saved through Jesus Christ.

MAJOR EVENTS:

The sin of all people: Paul expressed God's anger that the people chose to disobey God and lead sinful lives. He said that God will punish those who sin and don't come to him for his forgiveness. But there is hope. Because of God's amazing love, he offers eternal life and salvation through his son, Jesus Christ. *(Romans 1-3)*

Obedience to God: Paul explains that Christians are to follow God and to lead lives that are different from the world. *"Do not conform any longer to the pattern of this world, but be transformed by the renewing of your mind. Then you will be able to test and approve what God's will is — his good, pleasing and perfect will." (Romans 12:1–2)*

God-given gifts: Paul encouraged the people to use their God-given gifts to serve him and to show others about God's love: *"We have different gifts, according to the grace given us. If a man's gift is prophesying, let him use it in proportion to his faith. If it is serving, let him serve; if it is teaching, let him teach; if it is encouraging, let him encourage; if it is contributing to the needs of others, let him give generously; if it is leadership, let him govern diligently; if it is showing mercy, let him do it cheerfully."* All these gifts are to be used to help people come to know Jesus. *(Romans 12:6–8)*

1 CORINTHIANS

AUTHOR:
Paul

KEY SCRIPTURE:
Love is patient. Love is kind. It does not envy, it does not boast, it is not proud. It is not rude, it is not self-seeking, it is not easily angered, it keeps no record of wrongs. Love does not delight in evil but rejoices with the truth. It always protects, always trusts, always hopes, always perseveres. Love never fails. *1 Corinthians 13:4–8*

WHAT THIS BOOK IS ABOUT:
The apostle Paul started the church in Corinth, but the people were not living for God. So Paul wrote this letter to encourage and help the church put their trust in Jesus and to love one another.

MAJOR EVENTS:
The church divided: The church in Corinth was in the capital of Achaia, which is currently Greece. It was a large and busy city. The church was struggling because the people were focusing on their differences. Some were rich; some were poor. Paul tried to encourage the Corinthians to seek power and wisdom from God in all things. *(1 Corinthians 1:10 thru 5:13)*

Corinth, The Bema;
Ceremonial platform used for public speeches. Believed to be the place where Paul addressed the Corinthians.

True Love!

"Barbara Manatee,
you are the one for me!
Sent from up above,
you are the one I love!
Barbara Manatee,
I'll be your mon ami!
I'll take you to the ball,
I hope you're not
too tall."

Via Dolorosa;
Commemorates Christ's fall while carrying the cross - (Christ carries our burdens)

How to love: In 1 Corinthians 13, Paul tells believers how to love each other. *"Love is patient, love is kind. It does not envy, it does not boast, it is not proud. It is not rude, it is not self-seeking, it is not easily angered, it keeps no record of wrongs. Love does not delight in evil but rejoices with the truth. It always protects, always trusts, always hopes, always perseveres"* (vv. 4–7).

Coins;
Silver coins
from Corinth

2 CORINTHIANS

AUTHOR:
Paul

KEY SCRIPTURE:
Therefore, if anyone is in Christ, he is a new creation; the old has gone, the new has come! *2 Corinthians 5:17*

WHAT THIS BOOK IS ABOUT:
It takes courage to be a Christian and to treat others with respect and forgiveness.

MAJOR EVENTS:

Paul teaches: Paul asked the people to try to forgive one another. He encouraged them not to lose heart, but to be courageous and boldly rely on God for their needs, because when we turn our lives over to God, we are promised a wonderful life in heaven. *(2 Corinthians 1:1 thru 5:10)*

Give to the poor: Paul encouraged the people to give to the needy. He asked each of them to test the sincerity of their love by doing this. *(2 Corinthians 8:1–15)*

AUTHOR:

Paul

KEY SCRIPTURE:

I have been crucified with Christ and I no longer live, but Christ lives in me. The life I live in the body, I live by faith in the Son of God, who loved me and gave himself for me. *Galatians 2:20*

WHAT THIS BOOK IS ABOUT:

Paul wrote this letter to the church in Galatia that included Jews and Gentiles (people who were not Jewish). Paul talks about the difference between the law and grace. Paul wanted the people to understand that living a good life did not mean anything without the love and dedication to the Lord and the change that takes place when we become a new creation in Christ.

MAJOR EVENTS:

The gospel: Paul warned the people not to turn from the gospel of Christ. He reminded the people that Jesus was crucified for their sins and that each of them was baptized through faith and as such, was an heir to Christ's promise. *(Galatians 1:1 thru 4:20)*

Live by the Spirit: Paul taught the Galatians to let the Holy Spirit work through them to lead them away from their sinful desires. He told the people to live and be guided by godly character, called the fruit of the Spirit. *(Galatians 5:16–26)*

The fruit of the Spirit: The fruit of the Spirit is love, joy, peace, patience, kindness, goodness, faithfulness, gentleness, and self-control.

SPIRITUAL FRUIT!

Every fourth Tuesday at quarter past nine, the tower will shimmy and rattle and whine. And as the town nibbles on biggle bag fruits, a shiny new Snoodle will drop from a chute.

Be STRONG in THE LORD!

The Snoodle laughed as he leaped and ran from the cave, feeling now older and stronger and brave!

Ephesus, Odeum;
The Odeum in Ephesus, Western Turkey, 1st century A.D.

Carry each other's burdens: Paul encouraged the Galatians to help one another, to share, and to not think they were better than the next person. He told them to "become weary in doing good." *(Galatians 6)*

ephesians

AUTHOR:
Paul, while in prison

KEY SCRIPTURE:
There is one body and one Spirit—just as you were called to one hope when you were called—one Lord, one faith, one baptism—one God and Father of all, who is over all and through all and in all. *Ephesians 4:4–6*

WHAT THIS BOOK IS ABOUT:
Paul wrote this letter to the church in Ephesus, which is now called Turkey. He divided his letter into two sections. The first section talks about our part in God's eternal purpose. In the second part, Paul teaches ways that we can fulfill God's purpose by walking in his ways. Paul wanted the people to know what they need to become

true sons of God. In Ephesians 5:1–2 he teaches, "*Be imitators of God, therefore, as dearly loved children and live a life of love, just as Christ loved us and gave himself up for us as a fragrant offering and sacrifice to God.*" Paul wanted to equip the church and the people to overcome daily struggles through their faith in Christ Jesus. He teaches that we should put on an armor of God to combat temptation. He describes that armor in Ephesians 6:10–17:

Finally, be strong in the Lord and in his mighty power. Put on the full armor of God so that you can take your stand against the devil's schemes. For our struggle is not against flesh and blood, but against the rulers, against the authorities, against the powers of this dark world and against the spiritual forces of evil in the heavenly realms. Therefore put on the full armor of God, so that when the day of evil comes, you may be able to stand your ground, and after you have done everything, to stand. Stand firm then, with the belt of truth buckled around your waist, with the breastplate of righteousness in place, and with your feet fitted with the readiness that comes from the gospel of peace. In addition to all this, take up the shield of faith, with which you can extinguish all the flaming arrows of the evil one. Take the helmet of salvation and the sword of the Spirit, which is the word of God.

PHILIPPIANS

AUTHOR:
Paul, while in prison

KEY SCRIPTURE:
I can do everything through him who gives me strength. *Philippians 4:13*

WHAT THIS BOOK IS ABOUT:
Paul encourages the people to take joy in suffering, serving, believing, and giving. Suffering for Jesus is a privilege. Paul concludes in Philippians 4:4 by telling the people, "*Rejoice in the Lord always. I will say it again: Rejoice!*"

Philippi, Greece;
Ruins of the ancient city Philippi, in Northern Greece. Paul visited the city during his first mission and was imprisoned.

MAJOR EVENTS:

Be joyful!: Paul sent a message of joy to the people in Philippi:

Be joyful in suffering: He encouraged the people to continue a strong prayer life and always be thankful. He said that everything that happened to him helped to spread the word of Jesus Christ, so for that he was very joyful! Paul teaches that it is far better to suffer for Christ in this life and look forward to the eternal life with Christ in the future, as a reward. *(Philippians 1)*

Serve others: Paul talks about the joy in serving others. Paul says that instead of looking out for our own interests, we should look out for the interests of others. *(Philippians 2)*

Guard your mind: Paul helped believers put good things in their minds. *"Finally, brothers, whatever is true, whatever is noble, whatever is right, whatever is pure, whatever is lovely, whatever is admirable—if anything is excellent or praiseworthy—think about such things." (Philippians 4:8)*

Don't worry: Paul also plead with the people to not worry about anything! Instead, he told the Philippians to pray and trust God. *(Philippians 4:6–7)*

COLOSSIANS

AUTHOR:
Paul

KEY SCRIPTURE:
Therefore, as God's chosen people, holy and dearly loved, clothe yourselves with compas-

Pater Noster Church;
Located on the Mt. of Olives, the Lord's Prayer is written in more than fifty languages in the cloister of the monastery.

sion, kindness, humility, gentleness and patience. Bear with each other and forgive whatever grievances you may have against one another. Forgive as the Lord forgave you. And over all these virtues put on love, which binds them all together in perfect unity. *Colossians 3:12–14*

WHAT THIS BOOK IS ABOUT:

Paul urged the church at Colosse to depend only on the power and person of Jesus. Paul teaches how people should live as Christians individually, as a family, at work, and in our relationships with one another.

MAJOR EVENTS:

Who Jesus is: Paul reminded the people who Jesus is—the image of God, the firstborn of all creation, that all things have been created through him and for him, all things hold together in him, and that he is the head of the church. Jesus is above all things, and no one can compare to him. *(Colossians 1:1 thru 2:7)*

Hold fast: The people were told to only believe in Jesus and not any other teaching. *(Colossians 2:8 thru 2:23)*

Rules for Christian homes: Paul teaches wives how to treat their husbands, husbands how to treat their wives, and children to obey their parents. *(Colossians 3:18–20)*

1 Thessalonians

AUTHOR:
Paul

KEY SCRIPTURE:
Be joyful always, pray continually, give thanks in all circumstances; for this is God's will for you in Christ Jesus. *1 Thessalonians 5:16–18*

WHAT THIS BOOK IS ABOUT:
Paul's first letter to the Thessalonians was to provide support for those who were struggling with misunderstandings about Jesus Christ. He also provides direction for living a holy life. And, he writes regarding Jesus' second coming and of heaven.

FLYING HORSES!

"You're more likely to teach a horse to fly than to teach a city to love. That's what I used to think before I met Cavis and Millward on Christmas Eve. We learned that love really means giving up something for someone when they don't deserve it; when there's nothing in it for you. That's love!"

Kavalla, Greece;
Modern port of the ancient Roman city of Neapolis, in the Greek region of Macedonia. Paul started his mission to northern Greece from here.

MAJOR EVENTS:

Be faithful: Paul encouraged the people to be faithful to God. He remembered to pray every-day for them. *(1 Thessalonians 1:2–3)*

Lives that please: Paul instructed the people that they should be respectful of others, work hard, be joyful, live peacefully, show kindness, and pray all the time *(1 Thessalonians 4:11–12; 5:12–18)*

2 THessaLonians

AUTHOR:

Paul

KEY SCRIPTURE:

May the Lord direct your hearts into God's love and Christ's perseverance. *2 Thessalonians 3:5*

WHAT THIS BOOK IS ABOUT:

Paul wrote this book to encourage the people who lived in Thessalonia to tell others about Christ. This book also helps believers understand about Jesus' second coming.

MAJOR EVENTS:

Christ's return: Paul urged the people to stand firm in their beliefs and keep trusting and obeying until Jesus returns. *(2 Thessalonians 1:1 thru 3:5)*

Warning: Paul warned the people to stay away from those believers who did not follow the gospel and obey its teaching. He instructed the church to work hard and not be lazy or tire of doing good. *(2 Thessalonians 3:6–16)*

1 TiMOTHY

AUTHOR:
Paul

KEY SCRIPTURE:
Don't let anyone look down on you because you are young, but set an example for the believers in speech, in life, in love, in faith and in purity.
1 Timothy 4:12

WHAT THIS BOOK IS ABOUT:
Paul wrote these letters to Timothy, a pastor in a church at Ephesus, who was a new leader preaching the gospel of Christ. He encouraged Timothy to remain strong in his faith.

MAJOR EVENTS:
Instructions: Paul provided Timothy with instructions to help him lead the church.

Instructions about false teachings: Paul warned Timothy to be on guard against those trying to teach false messages about the gospel of Jesus Christ. *(1 Timothy 1:3–20)*

Instructions for leaders: Paul provided Timothy with a picture of what the church should be—a community of people who love each other well and who live lives of purity and excellence in their culture. *(1 Timothy 4:1 thru 5:24)*

Ephesus, Harbor Road;
Ancient road leading to the harbor.

ephesus!

Did you know that you can visit Ephesus today? It is located in the southwestern corner of Turkey and is known for being the best-preserved classical city on the Mediterranean.

2 TiMOTHY

AUTHOR:
Paul

KEY SCRIPTURE:
All Scripture is God-breathed and is useful for teaching, rebuking, correcting and training in righteousness, so that the man of God may be thoroughly equipped for every good work. *2 Timothy 3:16–17*

WHAT THIS BOOK IS ABOUT:
Paul's second letter to Timothy was most likely his last message, as he was imprisoned and near death. Timothy was responsible for a group of churches. Paul gave Timothy specific instructions for leading the churches and encouragement to be passionate for God.

TiTUS

AUTHOR:
Tradition says Paul.

KEY SCRIPTURE:
For the grace of God that brings salvation has appeared to all men. It teaches us to say "No" to ungodliness and worldly passions, and to live self-controlled, upright and godly lives in this present age, while we wait for the blessed hope—the glorious appearing of our great God and Savior, Jesus Christ, who gave himself for us to redeem us from all wickedness and to purify for himself a people that are his very own, eager to do what is good. *Titus 2:11–14*

WHAT THIS BOOK IS ABOUT:
Paul wrote this letter to Titus, whom he traveled with for a while on his missionary journey. Paul wanted to help Titus grow as a leader for the churches on an island called Crete. Paul talks about the qualifications for leaders of the church along with ways to live obediently for the Lord. There were very few people in Crete who knew about Jesus Christ, so Titus had a great responsibility to train new leaders for the church so that they could spread the good news in that region.

Crete art;
Fresco from the Minoan palace at Knossos

PHiLeMon

AUTHOR:
Paul

KEY SCRIPTURE:
I pray that you may be active in sharing your faith, so that you will have a full understanding of every good thing we have in Christ. *Philemon 1:6*

WHAT THIS BOOK IS ABOUT:
Paul wrote this letter to Philemon who had a slave named Onesimus. Onesimus ran away to Rome where he met Paul and became a Christian. Paul was sending Onesimus back to Philemon, as the law required, with this letter, asking Philemon to accept Onesimus back with forgiveness and love. In this letter Paul gives believers another example of how to love one another—to forgive even when it is not deserved.

HeBReWS

AUTHOR:
Unknown

KEY SCRIPTURE:
Now faith is being sure of what we hope for and certain of what we do not see. *Hebrews 11:1*

WHAT THIS BOOK IS ABOUT:
The letter to the Hebrews teaches that Jesus Christ is absolutely sovereign—greater than any priest who has ever lived. It points out that Christ must be the central focus of our faith. Therefore believers are to love each other as brothers and sisters, be kind to each other, and learn to be content. Hebrews 13:5 says, *"Keep your lives free from the love of money and be content with what you have, because God has said, 'Never will I leave you; never will I forsake you.'"*

Christians are to hold strong in our faith, trusting that the Lord will give us everything we need.

MAJOR EVENTS:

> *Christ is "greater than:"*
>
> **Christ is greater than angels.**
>
> **Christ is greater than Moses and all the prophets.**
>
> **Christ is greater than the Old Testament priesthood.**
>
> **The new covenant is greater than the old.**
>
> **Through Jesus we can be with God forever.**
>
> **Christ is perfect.**

Love one another!

If you see someone who's hurt or in need maybe it's time to perform a good deed. And when you've finished you'll find that it's true, when you make them feel better, you'll feel better too!

James

AUTHOR:
James, probably the James who was the brother of Jesus

KEY SCRIPTURE:
Who is wise and understanding among you? Let him show it by his good life, by deeds done in the humility that comes from wisdom. *James 3:13*

WHAT THIS BOOK IS ABOUT:
James wrote this letter to Christians to show what love-in-action looks like. Believers all know to love one another. This letter shows us how. He addresses everyday problems such as listening, anger, patience, sickness, temptation, selfishness, favoritism, and faith. James wanted to encourage the people to grow in faith and explained that their actions should be a direct result of their faith.

In James 1:22 he points out: *Do not merely listen to the word, and so deceive yourselves. Do what it says.*

MAJOR EVENTS:
Favoritism: James teaches that believers should not show favoritism. Those who are poor financially are often rich in faith. Christians are to love their neighbors as they love themselves. *(James 2:1-13)*

Faith and deeds: James explains that we are saved by grace through Jesus Christ, not by what we do. But faith causes us to do things for thers and work for Christ. *(James 2:14–26)*

Self-control: James instructed the people to be quick to listen to each other and slow to speak and slow to become angry. God wants believers to be careful of what they say and how they talk to others. *(James 1:19–20, 26)*

Wisdom: James urged believers to be careful in what they say and teach. We should also show our wisdom by what we do and how we act toward others. We should not envy or act selfishly toward others. *(James 3:13–18)*

1 PETER

AUTHOR:
Tradition says Peter.

KEY SCRIPTURE:
Humble yourselves, therefore, under God's mighty hand, that he may lift you up in due time. Cast all your anxiety on him because he cares for you. *1 Peter 5:6–7*

WHAT THIS BOOK IS ABOUT:
The Christians in Asia Minor were being persecuted (mistreated). Peter had great understanding of persecution. He was imprisoned and beaten for preaching God's Word, but through it all, he remained strong in his faith and tells the people that it is time to rejoice! Peter reminds the people how Christ suffered.

MAJOR EVENTS:
Be Holy: Peter encouraged the people to live a holy life, to exercise self-control, to stay obedient to God, and to have a sincere love toward one another. Peter says believers are God's chosen people, called out of darkness to his wonderful light. *(1 Peter 1:13 thru 2:10)*

Conduct: Peter encouraged the people to live obediently. He reminds us to live justly and lovingly as husband and wife. He wants us to live in harmony with one another, to be sympathetic, love as brothers, and be compassionate and humble. *(1 Peter 2:13 thru 3:7)*

When people are mean: Peter urged the believers to never repay evil with evil or insult with insult, but with blessing. *(1 Peter 3:9)*

Don't be afraid: Peter reminded Christians to share their faith. God does not want us to be afraid

Peter's House;
Archeological remains of Peter's house, Capernaum

John, Armenian Manuscript;
Opening page of the Evangelion Armenian
Illuminated Manuscript, 15th century

to tell others about him. Even if they laugh or say terrible things about us, we are to tell others the good news about Jesus. *(1 Peter 3:13–18)*

2 PETER

AUTHOR:
Tradition says Peter.

KEY SCRIPTURE:
His divine power has given us everything we need for life and godliness through our knowledge of him who called us by his own glory and goodness. *2 Peter 1:3*

WHAT THIS BOOK IS ABOUT:
The second letter of Peter, like many of the books in the New Testament, warns Christians against false teaching. Some people were arguing over what the coming judgment would be. Peter says that the judgment will come, but that because God is patient and loving, God hasn't returned yet.

1 JOHN

AUTHOR:
John, the apostle

KEY SCRIPTURE:
Dear friends, let us love one another, for love comes from God. Everyone who loves is born of God and knows God. *1 John 4:7*

WHAT THIS BOOK IS ABOUT:
The first letter of John speaks about God's great love for us and how he wants his children to love each other. We are to show God's love by living lives that please him.

John warns people not to love the world or anything in it. God is love. In 1 John 3:1 John says, *How great is the love the Father has lavished on us, that we should be called children of God!* Believers are to love one another deeply in truth and action.

False teaching was common in the early church. John taught that the Holy Spirit will help believers know what is true and what is false.

SHEEP TIPPING!
Being a shepherd is a very hard job; especially if your sheep keep tipping over. I think that's how God must feel about all of us. We keep falling, but, like a good shepherd, he's always there to pick us up!

a Thankful Heart!

A thankful heart is a happy heart. I'm glad for what I have and that's an easy way to start. That's why I say thanks every day!

AUTHOR:
John, the apostle

KEY SCRIPTURE:
And this is love: that we walk in obedience to his commands. As you have heard from the beginning, his command is that you walk in love. *2 John 1:6*

WHAT THIS BOOK IS ABOUT:
False teaching in the church was a big problem because there was not a complete New Testament for people to use like we can today. Some people had started teaching that Jesus hadn't come as a man to earth. John tells the church to have nothing to do with such teachers. The true gospel is that Jesus is both fully God and fully human.

AUTHOR:
John, the apostle

KEY SCRIPTURE:
I have no greater joy than to hear that my children are walking in the truth. *3 John 1:4*

WHAT THIS BOOK IS ABOUT:
The third letter of John is written to Gaius—a believer who opens up his home to other Christians. Gaius is praised for giving hospitality and encouraged to continue doing so. The author of letter tells Gaius to "imitate what is . . . good" *(v. 11)* even in the face of those who disagree with him.

AUTHOR:
Tradition says Jude.

The Last Judgment;
Fresco from the Byzantine church Chora in Istanbul, 13th century

KEY SCRIPTURE:

Dear friends, although I was very eager to write to you about the salvation we share, I felt I had to write and urge you to contend for the faith that was once for all entrusted to the saints. *Jude 1:3*

WHAT THIS BOOK IS ABOUT:

The book of Jude is a short book—only twenty-four verses—that encourages the believers to not turn from the truth of the gospel of Jesus. False teaching was threatening the church, so they were urged to remain faithful and not fall away from Jesus.

AUTHOR:

John, the apostle

KEY SCRIPTURE:

Behold, I am coming soon! My reward is with me, and I will give to everyone according to what he has done. I am the Alpha and the Omega, the First and the Last, the Beginning and the End. *Revelation 22:12–13*

WHAT THIS BOOK IS ABOUT:

John writes this book to the seven churches in Asia—now Turkey. Using strong word pictures, he offers hope and counsel to the believers. John explains that many will be persecuted or die because they believe. But faith is more important than anything.

Jesus was at the beginning of time and will be alive for all time. Jesus is above all. Jesus is in control of all governments and kings and authorities. Though you may not see him with your eyes, you can know he is always with you. John talks about the glory of heaven and how wonderful it will be to live with God for eternity.

SECTION 3
it's about Time!

The Jet ion Molecular Machine!

Hey kids! Allow me to introduce you to J.I.M.M. (Jet Ion Molecular Machine). J.I.M.M. is my latest invention! Check out these drawings to see how he will take you on a wonderful trip through history. You'll start out at the very beginning of time as we know it — when God created the world. Then you'll zoom through the years that are recorded in the Bible. First, you'll zigzag through the Old Testament. Then, assuming we don't have any complications or technical malfunctions, you'll zip right through the New Testament too! Hold on tight — J.I.M.M.'s a crazy driver!

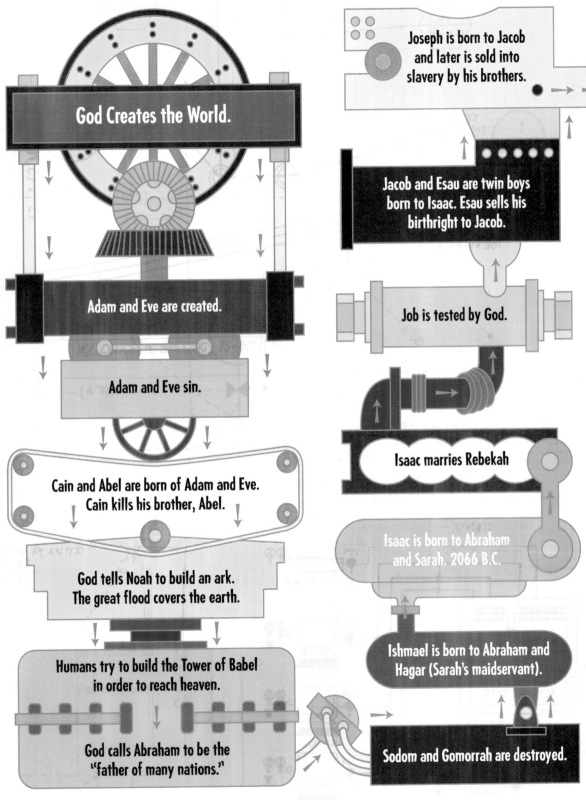

God Creates the World.

Adam and Eve are created.

Adam and Eve sin.

Cain and Abel are born of Adam and Eve. Cain kills his brother, Abel.

God tells Noah to build an ark. The great flood covers the earth.

Humans try to build the Tower of Babel in order to reach heaven.

God calls Abraham to be the "father of many nations."

Joseph is born to Jacob and later is sold into slavery by his brothers.

Jacob and Esau are twin boys born to Isaac. Esau sells his birthright to Jacob.

Job is tested by God.

Isaac marries Rebekah

Isaac is born to Abraham and Sarah. 2066 B.C.

Ishmael is born to Abraham and Hagar (Sarah's maidservant).

Sodom and Gomorrah are destroyed.

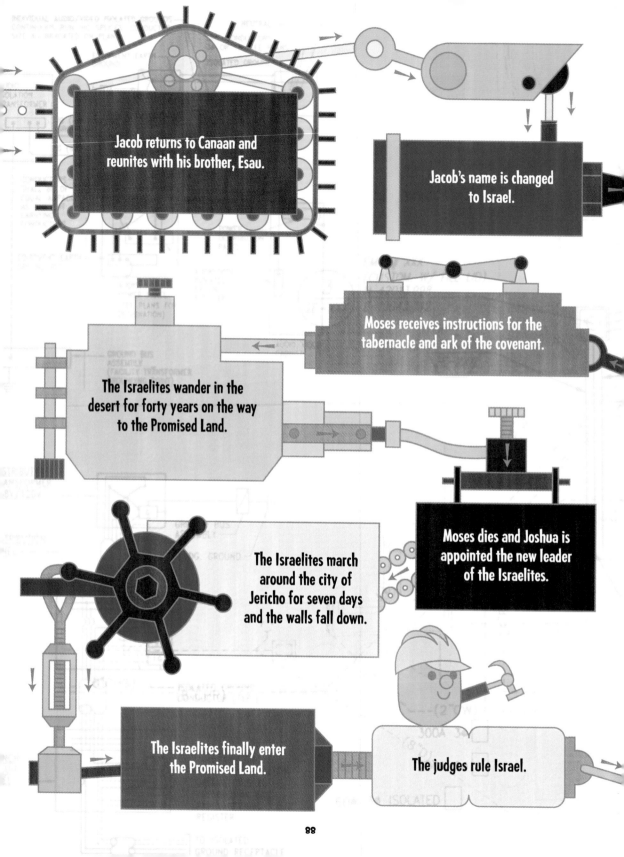

Jacob returns to Canaan and reunites with his brother, Esau.

Jacob's name is changed to Israel.

Moses receives instructions for the tabernacle and ark of the covenant.

The Israelites wander in the desert for forty years on the way to the Promised Land.

Moses dies and Joshua is appointed the new leader of the Israelites.

The Israelites march around the city of Jericho for seven days and the walls fall down.

The Israelites finally enter the Promised Land.

The judges rule Israel.

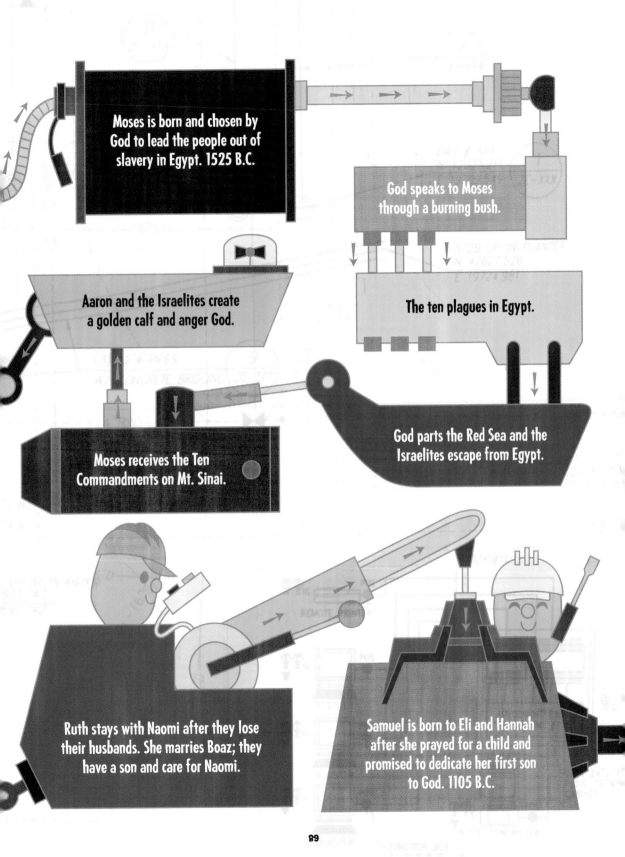

Moses is born and chosen by God to lead the people out of slavery in Egypt. 1525 B.C.

God speaks to Moses through a burning bush.

Aaron and the Israelites create a golden calf and anger God.

The ten plagues in Egypt.

Moses receives the Ten Commandments on Mt. Sinai.

God parts the Red Sea and the Israelites escape from Egypt.

Ruth stays with Naomi after they lose their husbands. She marries Boaz; they have a son and care for Naomi.

Samuel is born to Eli and Hannah after she prayed for a child and promised to dedicate her first son to God. 1105 B.C.

David and Jonathan become best friends. Saul tries to kill David.

David defeats the giant, Goliath. 1025 B.C.

David becomes a good and powerful king. 1003 – 970 B.C.

Saul becomes king and is anointed by the prophet Samuel. 1043 B.C.

David's son, Solomon, becomes king.

Solomon asks for wisdom.

As a child, Samuel hears God's voice speaking to him.

Solomon builds a glorious temple for God. 966 B.C.

Joel becomes a prophet and describes a swarm of locusts that descends upon Israel. 835 – 796 B.C.

Jonah refuses to deliver a message from God to Nineveh. He ends up in the belly of a fish and is spit out three days later. He then preaches the message from God to Nineveh. 785 – 753 B.C.

Obadiah becomes a prophet. 855 – 840 B.C. or 586 B.C.

Elisha tries to restore God's kingdom. 848 – 797 B.C.

Elijah leaves for heaven in a chariot of fire. 840 B.C.

Ahab and Jezebel lead the people to worship false gods. 870 B.C.

Elijah proves God against the prophets of Baal. 875 B.C.

The kingdom is divided after Solomon's death. The kingdom to the south is called Judah. The kingdom to the north becomes Israel. 930 B.C.

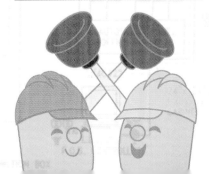

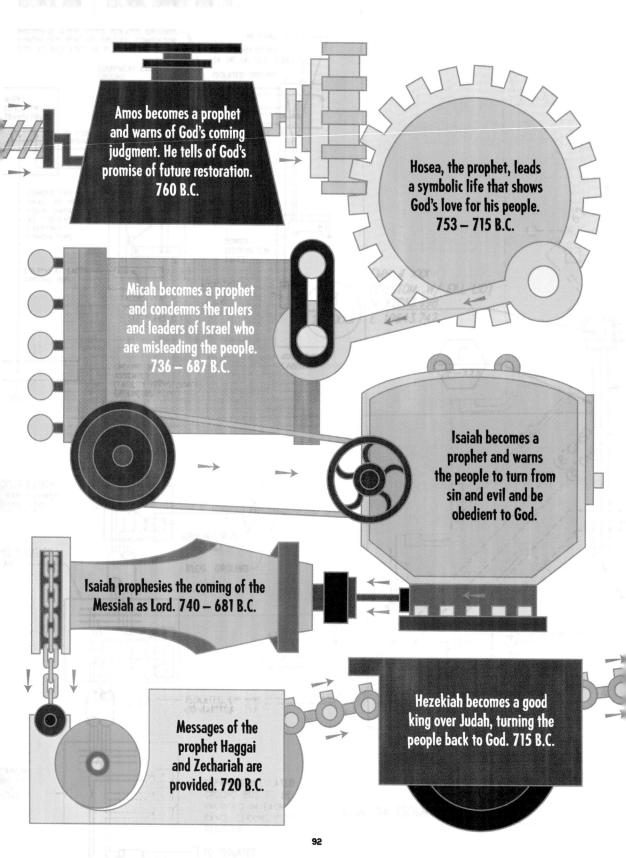

Amos becomes a prophet and warns of God's coming judgment. He tells of God's promise of future restoration. 760 B.C.

Hosea, the prophet, leads a symbolic life that shows God's love for his people. 753 – 715 B.C.

Micah becomes a prophet and condemns the rulers and leaders of Israel who are misleading the people. 736 – 687 B.C.

Isaiah becomes a prophet and warns the people to turn from sin and evil and be obedient to God.

Isaiah prophesies the coming of the Messiah as Lord. 740 – 681 B.C.

Messages of the prophet Haggai and Zechariah are provided. 720 B.C.

Hezekiah becomes a good king over Judah, turning the people back to God. 715 B.C.

All of Assyria is conquered. 609 B.C.

Ezekiel is taken captive in Babylon. 597 B.C.

Habakkuk, the prophet, complains about the world's injustice, not understanding why God allows his people to suffer. 619 – 589 B.C.

The fall of Nineveh. 612 B.C.

Jeremiah becomes a prophet and proclaims God has a plan and a future for his people. 627 – 586 B.C.

Josiah becomes the king of Judah at age eight. 640 B.C.

Zephaniah, the prophet, proclaims warnings of judgment along with encouragement. 640 – 621 B.C.

Nahum becomes a prophet and tells the Ninevites to turn away from evil and warns that they will be destroyed. 663 – 612 B.C.

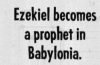

Ezekiel becomes a prophet in Babylonia.

Ezekiel proclaims a message of good news that God will restore the city. He assures that all of God's promises will be fulfilled. 593 – 571 B.C.

Haggai becomes a prophet to challenge the people in their faithfulness. He calls upon them to glorify God by building the temple. 520 B.C.

Esther saves the Jews by her courageous appearance before King Xerxes when she tells him that Haman has devised a plot to have the Jews killed. 474 B.C.

Zechariah becomes a prophet and continues to encourage the people to rebuild the temple. He also prophesies about the coming Messiah. 520 B.C.

Esther becomes a queen. 479 B.C.

Ezra ministers to Jerusalem. 458 B.C.

Jerusalem, the southern kingdom, falls. The people are exiled to Babylon, including Daniel, Shadrach, Meshach, and Abednego. 586 B.C.

Shadrach, Meshach, and Abednego refuse to bow down to the image of King Nebuchadnezzar and are thrown into a fiery furnace, but they are saved by God.

Daniel refuses to stop praying to God after a ruling made by King Darius, so he is thrown into a den of lions, but is saved by God.

Nehemiah comes to Jerusalem and the wall is completed. 445 B.C.

Malachi begins his ministry to warn the people not to turn away from God, but to be obedient. 430 B.C.

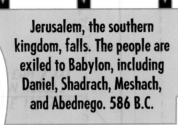

new Testament

Jesus is born in Bethlehem around 5 B.C.

Jesus visits the temple at age twelve.

John the Baptist begins his ministry preaching repentance from sin and telling about the Messiah.

Jesus is baptized.

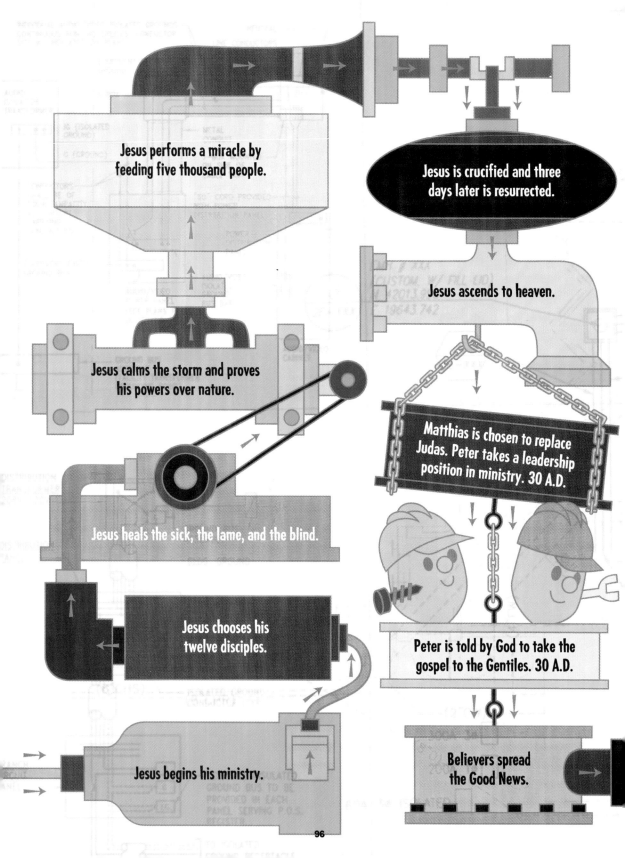

Jesus performs a miracle by feeding five thousand people.

Jesus is crucified and three days later is resurrected.

Jesus ascends to heaven.

Jesus calms the storm and proves his powers over nature.

Matthias is chosen to replace Judas. Peter takes a leadership position in ministry. 30 A.D.

Jesus heals the sick, the lame, and the blind.

Jesus chooses his twelve disciples.

Peter is told by God to take the gospel to the Gentiles. 30 A.D.

Jesus begins his ministry.

Believers spread the Good News.

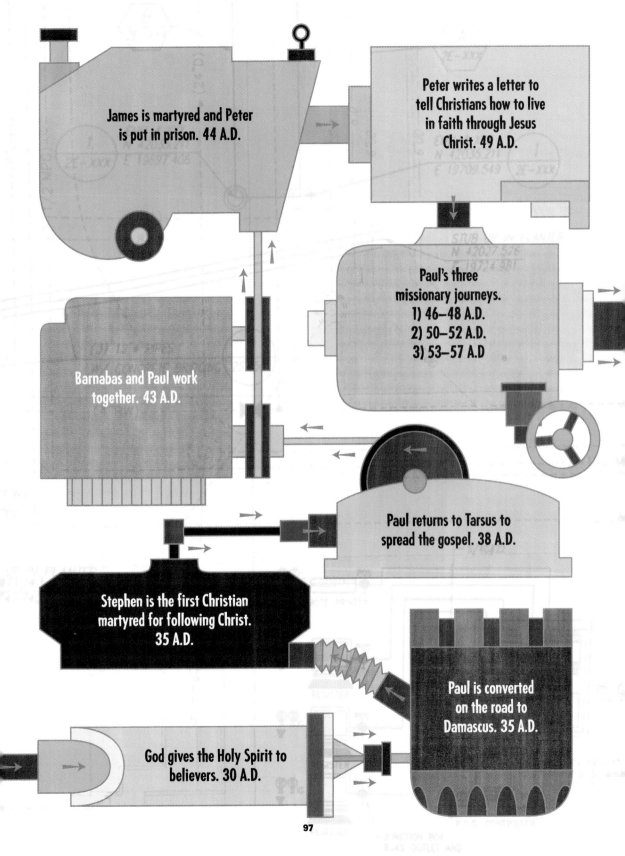

James is martyred and Peter is put in prison. 44 A.D.

Peter writes a letter to tell Christians how to live in faith through Jesus Christ. 49 A.D.

Paul's three missionary journeys.
1) 46–48 A.D.
2) 50–52 A.D.
3) 53–57 A.D

Barnabas and Paul work together. 43 A.D.

Paul returns to Tarsus to spread the gospel. 38 A.D.

Stephen is the first Christian martyred for following Christ. 35 A.D.

Paul is converted on the road to Damascus. 35 A.D.

God gives the Holy Spirit to believers. 30 A.D.

Paul writes letters to Ephesus, to the church in Colosse, and to Philemon.

Paul writes the people in Philippi to encourage them in joy. 61 A.D.

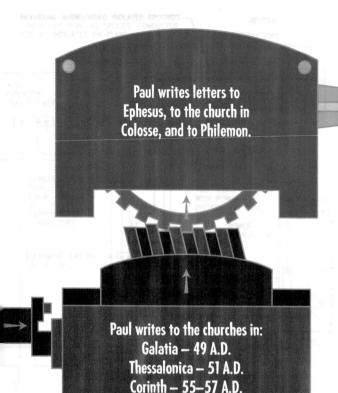

Paul writes to the churches in:
Galatia – 49 A.D.
Thessalonica – 51 A.D.
Corinth – 55–57 A.D.

Paul writes two letters to Timothy. He provides a foundation for the church leaders and warns against false teaching. 64–67 A.D.

Paul is imprisoned in Caesarea. 57–59 A.D.; Paul journeys to Rome. 59 A.D.; he is released from prison. 62 A.D.

Paul writes to the church in Rome to convey God's anger toward their sin. He also points them to the hope and salvation through Jesus Christ.

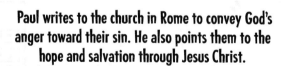

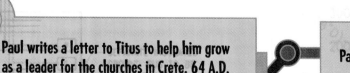

Paul writes a letter to Titus to help him grow as a leader for the churches in Crete. 64 A.D.

Paul is martyred. 67 A.D.

A letter is written to the Hebrews helping Jews see how Christ fulfilled the Jewish laws and prophecies. 70 A.D.

John writes 1, 2, and 3 John to teach Christians how to show love to each other. 85–90 A.D.

Rome destroys Jerusalem. 70 A.D.

Through a vision, John writes the book of Revelation and tells of the second coming of Christ and about heaven.

Jude writes a letter to Christians to encourage them in friendship and warn them to stay faithful.

As you can see, J.I.M.M. is really going to be pretty amazing! As soon as I finish putting up those shelves in my closet, and get the material from Nezzer's Hardware, I'm going to start building him. I hope you enjoyed the ride!

Peter writes two letters to the Christians in Asia Minor in hope of building them up in joy in the face of their persecution. 62–67 A.D.

SECTION 4

POWER TO THE PEOPLE!

WHO ARE ALL THESE PEOPLE?

Hello boys and girls! I'm so pleased that you could join me. I've spent hours, if not days, preparing for my part of the VeggieTales Atlapedia. My section is by far the most informative of them all; it is an in-depth review of the PEOPLE of the Bible. Within these pages, I am going to introduce you to some of the most interesting individuals in history. Who, by the way, had some of the craziest names that you've ever heard. I'll tell you about Shadrack, Belshazzar, Habakkuk, and Nebachadnezzar just to name a few. With names like that, they HAD to lead interesting lives. Don't you agree? Some of them made terrible mistakes, and others had amazing triumphs. Their stories are all recorded in the Bible, and this book will tell you who they were and where you can find their stories! Oh, come along now. Hurry, there's so much to tell!

Aaron the High Priest;
Illustation from a 16th-century German Manuscript

AARON *(Exodus 4–40; Leviticus 8)* Aaron was the brother of Moses. Aaron helped Moses with talking the king of Egypt into letting the Israelites leave that country. He was the very first high priest of Israel. Only men from his family could be priests.

ABEDNEGO *(Daniel 3)* Abednego was a good friend of Daniel who stood strong in his faith when King Nebuchadnezzar commanded the people to bow down and worship a false god. When Abednego and his friends, Shadrach and Meshach, refused to obey, the king threw them into a fiery furnace, but God saved them!

ABEL *(Genesis 4)* Abel was the second son born to Adam and Eve. Abel was a shepherd. His brother, Cain, was jealous of Abel. Cain killed Abel because God was pleased with Abel's sacrifice but not with Cain's.

ABIGAIL *(1 Samuel 25)* Abigail was married to Nabal. After he died, she married David. One of David's sisters was also named Abigail *(1 Chronicles 2:16–17)*.

Abraham Receives the Promise;
Wall painting from Dura Europos, one of the earliest known synagogues, dated 245 A.D.

ABRAHAM–ABRAM *(Genesis 11–25)* Abraham was first called Abram. He was chosen by God to become the father of the Jewish nation. He and his wife, Sarah, had no children, but God promised them a son. Abraham was one hundred years old, and

You Can Call Me Benny!

Rack, Shack, and I work real hard at the chocolate factory. We start at 8:00 and we don't get lunch 'til 3:00. We work the whole week through, to make a buck or two, so we can send them home to our families.

Adam Giving Names to the Animals;
Illustration from the Golden Hagada, dated 1320

Sarah was ninety when Isaac, the promised son, was born. God tested Abraham's faith by commanding him to sacrifice Isaac, the son he had waited so long for. Abraham showed his willingness to obey whatever God asked of him. God was pleased and saved Isaac before anything bad happened.

ADAM *(Genesis 1–2)* Adam was the first man God created. He was placed in the beautiful Garden of Eden with Eve where God gave them every-thing they needed. God asked just one thing of them—not to eat from the tree in the center of the garden. When Adam and Eve disobeyed and ate from the tree, sin entered the world.

AMOS *(Amos 1–9)* Amos was a shepherd from Judah and a prophet in Israel. There, Amos tried to convince the people how important it was to obey God. He warned them that God would punish them if they didn't do what God said.

ANANIAS *(Acts 4–5)* Ananias and his wife, Sapphira, sold some property to get money to give to the poor Christians, but they lied to Peter and the Holy Spirit about how much money they were giving. Because of their lies, they were punished and died.

ANANIAS *(Acts 9)* Ananias was a Christian disciple living in the city of Damascus. God told him to help Saul of Tarsus (who was later called Paul) af-ter he was made blind.

ANDREW *(Matthew 4; 10; John 1; 6; Acts 1)* Andrew was a fisherman chosen to be one of Jesus' twelve apostles. He brought his brother, Peter, to see Jesus. Later, Andrew brought a boy with a lunch to Jesus, and Jesus used it to feed over five thousand people.

AQUILA *(Acts 18; Romans 16:3–5; 1 Corinthians 16:19)* Aquila and his wife, Priscilla, were Jewish Christians who worked as tentmakers. They traveled with Paul to preach the good news of Jesus. They offered their home to the people for church worship.

BALAAM *(Numbers 22–24; 31; 2 Peter 2)* Balaam was a prophet from Midian who was hired by the king of Moab to come and curse the Israelites. On his way there, God caused Balaam's donkey to talk and an angel to

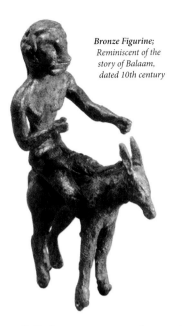

tell Balaam to say only good things about the Israelites.

BARABBAS *(Matthew 27; Mark 15; Luke 23; John 18)* Barabbas was a robber and a murderer who was in jail in Jerusalem when Jesus was arrested. When Pilate gave the Jewish people a choice about who to let go free, the people chose to free Barabbas and kill Jesus on the cross.

BARNABAS *(Acts 4; 13–15)* The apostles called him Barnabas, which means "one who encourages," because he helped others. Barnabas went with Paul on his first missionary trip, preaching the good news of Jesus.

BARTHOLOMEW *(Matthew 10; Luke 6; John 1)* Bartholomew, also known as Nathanael, was one of Jesus' twelve apostles. Philip brought him to see Jesus.

BATHSHEBA *(2 Samuel 11–12; 1 Kings 1–2)* Bathsheba was married to Uriah until David fell in love with her and had Uriah killed. Bathsheba and David also became the parents of Solomon.

BELSHAZZAR *(Daniel 5)* Belshazzar was an evil Babylon ruler where Daniel lived. During a banquet, a hand appeared and wrote a message from God on the wall. Daniel explained that the message meant that Belshazzar would be punished, and his kingdom would come to an end. That same night, Babylon was captured and Belshazzar was killed.

BENJAMIN *(Genesis 35; 42–45)* Benjamin was Jacob and Rachel's youngest son. His mother died when he was born, which made Jacob love Benjamin even more. His descendants became one of the twelve family tribes of Israel. King Saul and the apostle Paul were from Benjamin's family.

BOAZ *(Ruth 2–4)* Boaz was a wealthy, distant relative of Naomi's husband. After Naomi's husband and sons died, her daughter-in-law Ruth helped take care of Naomi. Ruth worked in Boaz's field to get the grain they needed. Later Boaz and Ruth married and became the great-grandparents of King David.

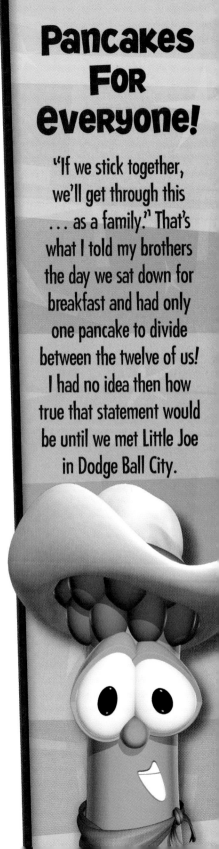

Pancakes For everyone!

"If we stick together, we'll get through this ... as a family." That's what I told my brothers the day we sat down for breakfast and had only one pancake to divide between the twelve of us! I had no idea then how true that statement would be until we met Little Joe in Dodge Ball City.

JeaLous Wisemen!

With God's help, Daniel explained my dreams to me and I was so thankful that I made him second in command of my kingdom. That's when his troubles began. The other wisemen were so angry that they convinced me to have Daniel thrown in a den of lions!

CAIAPHAS *(Matthew 26; John 11)* Caiaphas was the high priest who found Jesus guilty when he was arrested and tried in Jerusalem. Caiaphas sent Jesus to Pilate for his sentencing.

CAIN *(Genesis 4; 1 John 3)* Cain was the first son of Adam and Eve. He became jealous of his brother, Abel, and killed him. God punished Cain by making him wander for the rest of his life.

CALEB *(Numbers 13–14; Joshua 14)* Caleb was one of twelve spies that Moses sent to find out about the Promised Land of Canaan. Caleb and Joshua trusted God to help them take the land, and it happened forty years later.

CORNELIUS *(Acts 10)* Cornelius was a Roman centurion at Caesarea. He, his family, and several friends were among the first non-Jewish people to become Christians.

DANIEL *(Daniel 1–2; 6)* Daniel, with God's help, explained King Nebuchadnezzar's dream and what the writing on the wall meant for Belshazzar. King Darius put Daniel in a den of lions when he refused to stop praying to God. But Daniel was faithful and God saved him.

DARIUS THE MEDE *(Daniel 6)* This ruler of Persia made Daniel an important leader under him. When other rulers became jealous of Daniel, they convinced Darius to command that no one pray to anyone else but him. Daniel continued to pray to God, and although he

The Death of Abel;
And it came to pass. . . Cain rose up against his brother Abel, and slew him. **Genesis 4:8** *KJV*

didn't want to, Darius threw him in a den of lions. When God saved Daniel, King Darius was pleased and ordered everyone to worship Daniel's God!

DAVID *(1 Samuel 16–1 Kings 2; 1 Chronicles 11–29)* David was the son of Jesse and served his father as a shepherd. When a giant threatened the Israelites and said bad things about God, David volunteered to fight the giant. With God's help, he killed Goliath, the giant with a stone in a sling! David grew up to become a great leader. He was a writer, a poet, a musician, a war general, and the greatest king of Israel. Jesus was a descendant of David.

DEBORAH *(Judges 4–5)* Deborah was the only woman judge in Israel. She asked Barak to lead Israel's army against a Canaanite king named Jabin and his army commander, Sisera. With God's help, the Israelites were victorious.

DELILAH *(Judges 16)* Delilah was a Philistine woman whom Samson loved. The Philistines paid her to find out what made Samson strong. Samson finally told her that the secret of his strength was his hair, which had never been cut. While he was asleep, she had his hair cut.

DINAH *(Genesis 30; 46)* Dinah was the only daughter born to Jacob. She had twelve brothers.

DORCAS *(Acts 9)* Dorcas was also called Tabitha. She was a Christian who helped people by making clothes for them. When she died, her friends called for the apostle Peter to come. Through God's help, Peter raised her from death.

ELI *(1 Samuel 1–4)* Eli was a priest and a judge of Israel for forty years. His sons were disobedient to God. Eli trained Samuel how to speak to and listen to God so he could take his place as the judge of Israel.

ELIJAH *(1 Kings 17; 2 Kings 1–2)* Elijah was a prophet during the time of King Ahab, about eight hundred years before Jesus was born. He was a good man who tried to get the Israelites to worship God instead of the idol Baal. Elijah did not die but was taken up to heaven in a whirlwind.

ELISHA *(1 Kings 19; 2 Kings 2–13)* Elisha took Elijah's place as Israel's prophet. God gave him power to heal sickness and raise people from death. Elisha told the people God's message for more than fifty years.

ELIZABETH *(Luke 1)* Elizabeth was the wife of the priest, Zechariah. She was the mother of John the Baptist. She was also related to Mary, the mother of Jesus.

Giant Pickles!

The Bible says that the Israelites were God's chosen people, but yet when they were faced with the task of fighting Goliath, the children of God were very afraid. They forgot that if God was on their side, no one could stand against them... But then Dave reminded them with a slingshot and a single stone.

I didn't even want to be queen. But Mordechi told me that God had to have a reason for making me queen of Persia. Then when the king banished my cousin Mordecai to the Island of Perpetual Tickling, I knew what that reason was.

Elijah on Mt. Carmel;
Wall painting from Dura Europos, dated 245 A.D.

ESAU *(Genesis 25; 27–28; 32–33)* Esau was Isaac and Rebekah's oldest son and Jacob's twin brother. One day Esau came back from hunting and was so hungry he sold his birthright to his brother Jacob in exchange for a bowl of stew. Later, he was tricked out of his father's blessing by Jacob and their mother, Rebekah. Esau finally forgave Jacob and they were friends as well as brothers.

ESTHER *(book of Esther)* Esther was a Jewish orphan who became the wife of King Xerxes of Persia. That made her the queen. Her cousin, Mordecai, told her that the king's most important assistant was planning to kill all the Jews. Esther showed great courage by risking her life to save her people.

EVE *(Genesis 2–4)* Eve was the first woman that God created from one of Adam's ribs. She and Adam were placed in the beautiful Garden of Eden where God gave them everything they needed. Eve disobeyed God by eating the fruit from the tree in the center of the garden. She gave some to Adam and he ate it. When they disobeyed, sin entered the world.

EZEKIEL *(book of Ezekiel)* Ezekiel was a Jewish prophet who explained to the people that God used the Babylonians to punish the Jews for their disobedience. But he also gave them a message of hope that they would one day go back to Jerusalem.

EZRA *(book of Ezra; Nehemiah 8)* Ezra was a Jewish priest and teacher of the Law of Moses. Ezra led a group of Jews who were allowed to leave Babylon and go back to Jerusalem. There he worked with Nehemiah to reestablish the Law and taught the people how to worship and serve God.

GABRIEL *(Daniel 8–9; Luke 1)* Gabriel is God's angel who appeared four times in the Bible. He appeared twice to Daniel to tell him what a vision meant. He also appeared twice in the New Testament when he announced that John the Baptist and Jesus would be born.

GAIUS *(Romans 16; 1 Corinthians 1; 3 John)* Gaius was a Christian who lived in Corinth. The apostle Paul stayed with him, and the church met in his house. He is also thought to be the same Gaius known for helping traveling preachers whom John wrote his third letter to.

GIDEON *(Judges 6–8)* Gideon was a judge of Israel. God called Gideon to lead Israel's army of only three hundred men to defeat the Midianites, their enemy; which they did with God's help.

GOD *(Genesis–Revelation)* God is the Father and Creator of the universe. God made everyone and everything in it. God has always been alive, and he will never die. God is all-wise, all-powerful, and all-loving. God loves us so much that he

sent his Son Jesus to take our punishment for our sins. God is perfect and he is love. He wants his people to believe and obey Jesus. When they do, they can live forever with God.

David and Goliath;
Hebrew manuscript, Florence 1460

GOLIATH *(1 Samuel 17; 1 Chronicles 20)* Goliath was the giant Philistine who was nine feet four inches tall. He challenged the Israelites to fight. Everyone was afraid of him except David. With God's help, David killed Goliath with just one stone in a sling.

GOMER *(Hosea 1)* Gomer was the unfaithful wife of the prophet, Hosea. God used her to teach Israel about their relationship to God.

HABAKKUK *(book of Habakkuk)* Habakkuk was a prophet during the reign of King Josiah.

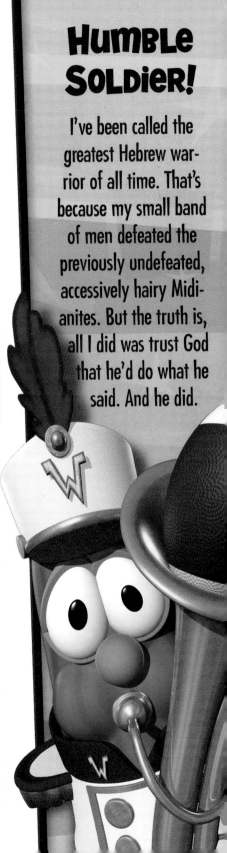

HUMBLE SOLDIER!

I've been called the greatest Hebrew warrior of all time. That's because my small band of men defeated the previously undefeated, accessively hairy Midianites. But the truth is, all I did was trust God that he'd do what he said. And he did.

Sneaky Matters of the King!

In order to protect my position as second in command of Persia, I devised a brilliant plan to have Mordecai and his whole sneaky family banished to the Island of Perpetual Tickling. I just didn't know that the queen was a member of that family... sneaky, very sneaky.

God told Habakkuk that he would send the Babylonians to destroy Jerusalem and punish the people.

HAGGAI *(Ezra 5; book of Haggai)* Haggai was the first prophet to prophesy in Palestine after the Jews returned to Jerusalem from Babylon. He encouraged the Israelites to finish rebuilding the temple.

HAM *(Genesis 7; 9–10; 1 Chronicles 1)* Ham was one of Noah's sons. He, his wife, his parents, his brothers, and their wives were saved in the ark during the Flood, along with the animals. The descendants of Ham settled in an area from Babylon to Egypt which included Canaan.

HAMAN *(Esther 3–9)* Haman was the chief officer for the king of Persia. He hated a Jew named Mordecai, so he lied and plotted to have the Jews killed. Queen Esther, who was a Jew, found out and told the king about Haman's plot. The king had Haman hung on the same gallows he had built to hang Mordecai.

HANNAH *(1 Samuel 1–2)* Hannah promised God that if he gave her a son, she would let him serve in the Lord's house. God blessed her with a boy whom she named Samuel. Hannah kept her promise to God and took him to the Holy Tent where Samuel was trained by the priest Eli.

HEROD THE GREAT *(Matthew 2; Luke 1)* Herod the Great was the king of Palestine when Jesus was born. Herod was frightened that the baby "king of the Jews" would grow up and take away his throne. So he ordered that all boy babies under two be killed, but God kept Jesus safe.

HEROD AGRIPPA I *(Acts 12)* Herod Agrippa I was the grandson of Herod the Great, and nephew of Herod Antipas. He had the apostle James killed and arrested the apostle Peter. He was eaten by worms and died because he let the people worship him as a god.

HEROD ANTIPAS *(Matthew 14; Luke 23)* Herod Antipas is the son of Herod the Great. He had John the Baptist put in prison and beheaded. Pilate sent Jesus to him for trial, because he came from Herod's territory in Galilee.

HEZEKIAH *(2 Kings 18–20; 2 Chronicles 29–32)* Hezekiah was a good king of Judah when Isaiah prophesied. Hezekiah believed in the one, true God and reopened the temple. He got rid of the idols the people worshiped.

HOLY SPIRIT *(Genesis–Revelation)* The Holy Spirit is one of the three persons of God. The other two are God the Father and God the Son, Jesus. The Holy Spirit

Herod's Temple;
Model of Herod's temple in Jerusalem. The temple was a fifty mile high marble building and sheltered the holy ark, the golden altar, and the golden menorah.

helped with the creation of the world, helped the apostles do miracles, and led men to write God's Word, the Bible. The Holy Spirit is also called the Spirit of God, the Spirit of Christ, the Spirit of Truth, the Comforter, and the Counselor. The Holy Spirit lives in Christians today and helps them understand God's will and obey him.

HOSEA *(book of Hosea)* Hosea was a prophet of Israel who lived about seven hundred years before Jesus. He was married to a woman who was unfaithful to him, but he loved her anyway. In his book, God told Hosea that his love for Israel was like Hosea's love for his wife. God wanted his people to love him and come back to him and know of his steadfast love for them.

HULDAH *(2 Kings 22; 2 Chronicles 34)* Huldah was a woman prophet who lived in Jerusalem. When Josiah was king in Judah, he had the temple repaired. A scroll of the Law was found in the ruins. Josiah sent the priest and four other men to Huldah, and she told them what it was.

ISAAC *(Genesis 21-26)* Isaac was the promised son of Abraham and Sarah. His name means laughter, because Sarah laughed when she heard the angel tell Abraham that they would have a son. When Isaac was a young boy, Abraham obeyed God and was willing to give Isaac as a sacrifice to God. Isaac later married Rebekah and became the father of Esau and Jacob.

Abraham prepares to sacrifice Isaac;
Mosaic floor of the 6th-century synagogue in Beth-Alpha

ISAIAH (2 Kings 19–20; book of Isaiah)

Isaiah was a Jewish prophet who told the people of Judah that God would punish them for their disobedience, but then better times would come. His words about Jesus' coming are often quoted in the New Testament.

ISSACHAR (Genesis 30; 49; Numbers 1; Judges 5)

Issachar was the ninth of Jacob's twelve sons. His descendants became the Israelite tribe of Issachar.

JACOB (Genesis 25–50; Matthew 1; 8; John 4)

Jacob was one of the sons of Isaac and Rebekah. He was Esau's younger twin who bought his birthright from him. Jacob had twelve sons and one daughter and became the father of the Jewish nation. Each son became the head of a family group or tribe. His name was changed to Israel, and the twelve family tribes were known as the Israelites.

JAMES (Matthew 13; Acts 12; 21)

James was a brother of Jesus and most likely wrote the book of James. After Jesus' res-

Isaac Blessing Jacob;
Illustration from the Golden Hagada, dated 1320

urrection, he became a strong leader of the new church.

JAMES, son of Alphaeus (Matthew 10; Mark 3; Acts 1)

This James was one of Jesus' twelve apostles. He is sometimes called James the Less because he was either younger than the other disciple named James, or because he was a small man.

JAMES, son of Zebedee (Matthew 4; 10; Luke 9; Acts 12)

James was a son of Zebedee and brother of John. Like his father and brother, James was a fisherman. He was one of Jesus' twelve apostles. James, John, and Peter were Jesus' closest friends. James was killed by Herod Agrippa I.

JAPHETH (Genesis 6–7; 9–10; 1 Chronicles 1)

Japheth was one

Church of St. James;
Built in 1160 on the site where James was killed.

of Noah's three sons. He and his wife were saved in the ark during the Flood. Japheth's descendants are the Gentiles.

JEREMIAH *(2 Chronicles 35–36; Jeremiah 1–2; 36–40)* Jeremiah was a faithful prophet who was not liked because he warned the people that they would be punished because they disobeyed God. He had a hard life and was alive when Jerusalem was destroyed and the people were taken off to Babylon.

JESUS *(Genesis–Revelation)* Jesus is the second of the three persons of God. He, like the Father and the Holy Spirit, was there at the beginning of the creation of the world. He is in the Old Testament and New Testament. He is God's Son, but he was born to Mary in Bethlehem. The angel Gabriel told Mary and Joseph to name him Jesus because he would save the world from sin. Jesus grew up and lived a perfect life, and never sinned. He taught the people about God and his love. He showed them how important it is to obey God and follow only him. His miracles showed God's amazing power and compassion. He was killed by the Romans on a cross as a punishment for our sins. Three days later he came back from death, appeared to

Mister Grumpy Pants!

I traveled with Jonah all the way from the Pirates' ship to the belly of the whale and then on to Nineveh. Most of the time, he was a pretty grumpy traveling buddy. He refused to give the people of Nineveh a second chance. God wants us to give everyone a second chance.

several women and his disciples, and then rose up into heaven to be with his Father. If we follow and obey Jesus, we can live forever with him.

JETHRO *(Exodus 2–3; 18)* Jethro was faithful to God. He was a Midianite priest and the father of Moses' wife, Zipporah. When Moses led the Israelites out of Egypt, Jethro gave him advice about how to deal with the people in the desert.

Jezebel Opal;
Phoenician seal carved with several symbols and inscribed "YZBL," the Phoenician form of the name Jezebel.

JEZEBEL *(1 Kings 16; 18–21; 2 Kings 9)* Jezebel was the evil wife of Israel's King Ahab. She worshiped false gods and had many of God's prophets killed. Because she was so evil, the prophet Elijah told her she would die a horrible death, and she did.

JOANNA *(Luke 8; 24)* Joanna was a woman Jesus healed.

When Jesus was killed, Joanna was one of the women who prepared the spices for his burial.

JOB *(book of Job)* Job was a good and honest man who loved God. He lost everything he had—his family, his money, and his health. Although he did not know why it happened, Job remained faithful to God and was rewarded with even more than he started with.

JOEL *(book of Joel; Acts 2)* Joel was a prophet in Judah. He told them their enemies would come in like locusts and destroy everything. Joel wanted the people to change and obey God. He also talked about God's promise to send the Holy Spirit.

John the Baptist;
Mosaic from Hagi Sophia, Istambul, dated 9th century

JOHN THE BAPTIST *(Matthew 3; 11; 14; Luke 1; 3; 7)* John was the son of Elizabeth and Zechariah and was also related to Jesus. John was a prophet sent by God to tell the people that Jesus, the Messiah, was coming soon. He told them they should repent and be baptized. He lived out in the wilderness and ate locusts and honey. John baptized Jesus in the Jordan River. He was later put in prison and beheaded by Herod Antipas.

JOHN, the son of Zebedee *(Matthew 4; 10; 17; John 19; Acts 3-4; Revelation 1)* John was one of Jesus' twelve apostles. He was a fisherman, the son of Zebedee and the brother of James, the apostle. John was called "the disciple whom Jesus loved." Jesus asked John to care for his mother, Mary, after his death. John wrote the Gospel of John, 1, 2, 3 John, and the book of Revelation. He spent his life telling others about Jesus.

JONAH *(book of Jonah)* Jonah was a prophet whom God sent to deliver a message to the city of Nineveh. Jonah didn't want to. So he got on a boat sailing the opposite way. He was swallowed by a great fish that God sent, but was given a second chance when he was spit out by the fish three days later. He finally obeyed God and went to Nineveh to deliver the message. The people believed and obeyed God.

JONATHAN *(1 Samuel 13-14; 18-20; 31; 2 Samuel 1)* Jonathan was King Saul's son and a very good friend to David. Jonathan did whatever he could to help David in his relationship with King Saul.

JOSEPH *(Genesis 37-50; Exodus 1; 13; Acts 7)* Joseph was born to Jacob and Rachel. When he got older, his brothers were jealous of him. So they sold him as a slave to Egypt. He trusted God no matter what happened to him. God helped him explain Pharaoh's dreams. Pharaoh put Joseph in charge of saving food so there would be food during the coming drought. When his brothers came for food, he was able to save his family from hunger and forgive them.

JOSEPH OF ARIMATHEA *(Matthew 27; Mark 15)* This Joseph took the body of Jesus from the cross. He placed Jesus in his own new tomb he had cut out of the rock. Joseph was a member of the Sanhedrin and a disciple of Jesus.

JOSEPH OF NAZARETH *(Matthew 1-2; Luke 1-2)* Joseph married Mary, the mother of Jesus. He was a carpenter in Nazareth. The New Testament says he was a good man. After Jesus' childhood, the Bible doesn't say anymore about Joseph.

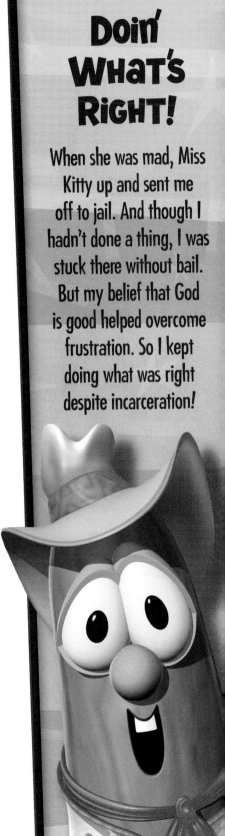

Doin' WHAT'S RiGHT!

When she was mad, Miss Kitty up and sent me off to jail. And though I hadn't done a thing, I was stuck there without bail. But my belief that God is good helped overcome frustration. So I kept doing what was right despite incarceration!

God's Way!

I know God's directions don't always make sense to us, but things work out a lot better when we do them God's way, instead of trying to do things our own way! When we remember that God made us and loves us, we can be sure that his way is always the best way.

JOSHUA *(Exodus 17; Deuteronomy 31; 34; book of Joshua)* Joshua was the leader of the Israelites after Moses died. He led the people into the Promised Land and helped them fight the battles. Joshua divided this land among the twelve tribes. At the end of his life, he told the people to choose whom they would serve—God or false gods.

JOSIAH *(2 Kings 22–23)* Josiah was only eight years old when he became king in Judah. He was a good king and wanted to obey God. He had the temple repaired where the workers found the Book of the Law of Moses. Josiah was very upset because the people had not been doing what God wanted and were going to be punished. But because Josiah wanted to obey God, God promised the punishment would come after Josiah had died.

JUDAH *(Genesis 29; Judges 1; 2 Samuel 2; Matthew 1; Luke 3; Revelation 5)* Judah was the fourth son of Jacob. It was Judah's idea to sell their brother Joseph as a slave to Egypt. Judah's descendants became the Israelite tribe of Judah. King David and Jesus were from his family.

JUDAS ISCARIOT *(Matthew 10; 26–27; John 12–13)* Judas was one of Jesus' twelve apostles. He turned Jesus over to the Romans to be killed. The chief priests paid Judas thirty pieces of silver for Jesus, the price of a slave. Later, Judas hanged himself because of his guilt.

JUDE *(John 7; book of Jude)* Jude was possibly a brother to Jesus and James. At first he did not believe that Jesus was God's Son. Later, he did believe and was a strong leader in the church. He wrote the book of Jude.

Raising of Lazarus;
Roman catacomb fresco, symboling the deliverance from death.

Hakel Dama;
Meaning "The Field of Blood," purchased by Judas with the money he received for betraying Jesus. Located south of Jerusalem.

LAZARUS *(John 11)* Lazarus was the brother of Mary and Martha. He lived in Bethany and was a very good friend to Jesus. When Lazarus got sick and died, Jesus brought him back to life.

LEVI *(Genesis 29; Exodus 6; Joshua 21)* Levi was the third of Jacob's twelve sons. His descendants became the Israelite tribe of Levi called Levites. Moses and Aaron were from Levi's family. All the priests who served at the temple were Levites.

LOT *(Genesis 13–14; 19)* Lot was Abraham's nephew who traveled with him to Canaan. He and his wife lived in Sodom, an evil city. God saved Lot by telling him and his family to run away and not look back until they got to the mountains. His wife, however, disobeyed. When she looked back, she was turned into a pillar of salt.

LUKE *(Colossians 4; 2 Timothy 4)* Luke was a well-educated doctor who spoke Greek. He traveled with the apostle Paul on some of his trips. Luke was the only non-Jewish author in the New Testament. He wrote the Gospel of Luke and the book of Acts.

LYDIA *(Acts 16; 40)* Lydia was a lady from the city of Thyatira. She sold purple cloth. Paul met her in the city of Philippi and told her about Jesus. She and the people who lived in her home were the first people on the continent of Europe to become Christians.

You Can Call Me Shack!

Rack, Benny, and I told Mr. Nezzer that our parents taught us to stand up for what we believe in and to always do what's right. And there was a lot of stuff in Mr. Nezzer's Bunny Song that was just not right. So we didn't sing it!

Mary with infant Jesus;
Mosaic from the Byzantine church Chora in Istambul, dated 13th century

MALACHI *(book of Malachi)* Malachi was a prophet during the time of Nehemiah. Malachi wrote the last book in the Old Testament. His message was for the people to obey God and trust him to take care of them. He told them that punishment would come, but that God still loved them.

MARK *(Acts 12–13; 15; Colossians 4; 2 Timothy 4)* Mark was also known as John Mark. He traveled with Paul and Barnabas on part of their first missionary journey. He also wrote the Gospel of Mark.

MARTHA *(Luke 10; John 11–12)* Martha was the sister of Mary and Lazarus. They all lived in Bethany. She was a good friend of Jesus and often opened her home to him when he would visit.

MARY *(Luke 10; John 11)* Mary was the sister of Martha and Lazarus. She sat at Jesus' feet and listened to him teach. To show how much she loved Je-

woman whom God chose to be the mother of Jesus. She married a man named Joseph, and they had other children. Mary was at the cross when Jesus was killed. After he went back to heaven, she met with the disciples to pray in Jerusalem.

MATTHEW *(Matthew 9–10; Mark 2; Luke 5)* Matthew was also known as Levi. He was a tax collector and one of Jesus' twelve apostles. He wrote the Gospel of Matthew.

MATTHIAS *(Acts 1)* Matthias was the apostle chosen to replace Judas. This was after Judas betrayed Jesus and then killed himself.

MESHACH *(Daniel 3)* Meshach was a good friend of Daniel. When King Nebuchadnezzar told the people to bow down and worship a statue, Meshach, Shadrach, and Abednego would not do that. The king threw them into a fiery furnace, but God saved them!

MICAH *(Micah 2–3; 5)* Micah was a prophet who told the people that God was displeased with them because they only pretended to worship him while they cheated others. But Micah also told them some good news. A great ruler would be born in Bethlehem. That was where Jesus was born about seven hundred years later.

sus, she poured some expensive perfume on his feet and dried them with her hair.

MARY MAGDALENE *(Matthew 27; Mark 15–16; Luke 8; John 19–20)* This Mary was from the town of Magdala in Galilee. After Jesus healed her, she was a dedicated follower. Mary was the first to see Jesus after he was raised from death.

MARY, mother of Jesus *(Matthew 1; Luke 1–2; John 19; Acts 1)* Mary was the very special

THE BIG SISTER!

Baby-sitting is really hard work, especially at feeding time. YUCK! I was getting really grumpy about having to watch my little brother every day. Then one day my big brother, Aaron, saved me from being run over by the princess's carriage. Then I realized what it means to be family. We take care of each other.

THE GOOD GUARD!

The Peoni brothers were the worst criminal minds in the kingdom... well, maybe the second worst next to Haman. When I saw them trying to smash the king with a piano, I had to help him. The Peoni brothers were caught and sent to the Island of Perpetual Tickling. I would hate to go there.

Mordecai and Esther;
Wall painting from Dura Europos, one of the earliest known synagogues, dated 245 A.D.

MIRIAM (*Exodus 2; 15; Numbers 12; 26; Micah 6*) Miriam was the sister of Moses and Aaron. Miriam watched over her baby brother Moses when their mother put his basket in the Nile River to save him from the evil king of Egypt. When the king's daughter found the basket, Miriam asked her if she wanted someone to care for baby Moses. The princess said yes and Miriam went and got her mother.

MORDECAI (*Esther 2–10*) Mordecai was a Jewish relative of Esther, who became the queen of Persia. When Mordecai discovered that the king's chief officer was planning to kill all of the Jews, he encouraged Esther to tell the king, even though it was dangerous. She told the king and saved the Jewish people, and the king made Mordecai his new chief officer.

MOSES (*books of Exodus, Leviticus, Numbers, and Deuteronomy; Hebrews 11*) Moses was brought up in the Egyptian court by his Hebrew mother. God spoke to Moses in a burning bush. He told Moses to lead the people from slavery in Egypt to the Promised Land. Through Moses, God parted the Red Sea so the Israelites could escape from the Egyptian army. God also gave Moses the Ten Commandments. Moses wrote the first five books of the Old Testament.

NAAMAN (*2 Kings 5*) Naaman commanded the Aramean army. He had a serious skin disease called leprosy and went to see the prophet Elisha. Elisha told him to wash seven times in the Jordan River. When he did as Elijah said, he was cured.

NAHUM *(book of Nahum)* Nahum was a prophet who warned the Ninevites that they would be punished because they had started doing bad things again. He wrote the book of Nahum in the Old Testament.

NAOMI *(book of Ruth)* Naomi was the mother-in-law of Ruth. After both their husbands had died, Ruth stayed with Naomi to care for her. Naomi introduced Ruth to Boaz. They got married and then both of them took care of Naomi.

NEBUCHADNEZZAR *(2 Kings 24–25; 2 Chronicles 36; Daniel 1–5)* Nebuchadnezzar was the king of Babylon who destroyed Jerusalem and took the people as captives. Daniel's friends, Shadrach, Meshach, and Abednego, were thrown into the fiery furnace because they wouldn't worship the statue he put up.

NEHEMIAH *(book of Nehemiah)* Nehemiah was a Hebrew in Persia who asked God to use him to help rebuild the city walls around Jerusalem. The people did it in only fifty-two days. Nehemiah served as a governor in Jerusalem. He helped the people know God's Word and encouraged them to obey God.

NICODEMUS *(John 3; 7; 19)* Nicodemus was a Pharisee and ruler of the Jews. Nicodemus came to learn from Jesus one night. After Jesus died, he helped to bury Jesus in the tomb.

NOAH *(Genesis 5–10; 1 Peter)* Noah was obedient to God during a time when everyone else had turned to evil. God told him to build an ark that saved his family and the animals from a great flood.

Mt. Ararat;
When the waters of the great flood receded, Noah's ark came to rest on the peak of Mt. Ararat.

Love The Bunny!

The bunny, the bunny, whoa, I love the bunny. I don't love my soup or my bread, just the bunny. The bunny, the bunny, yeah, I love the bunny. I gave everything that I had for the bunny. I don't want no buddies to come out and play. I'll sit on my sofa and eat bunnies all day!

Church of Saint Peter;
Fresco depicting St. Peter on the stormy Sea of Galilee

OBADIAH *(book of Obadiah)*
Obadiah was a prophet who told the people of Edom that God would punish them for not helping their relatives, the Israelites. The Edomites seemed to enjoy watching bad things happen to the Israelites. Obadiah wrote the book of Obadiah, the shortest book in the Old Testament.

PAUL *(Acts 7–28; Romans–Philemon)* Paul, who was first known as Saul, put Christians in jail and had them killed. Then Jesus came to him, and changed his life completely. Paul became an apostle of Je-sus to the Gentiles who started and strengthened churches. He made three long missionary trips teaching people about Jesus. Paul wrote Romans, 1 and 2 Corinthians, Galatians, Ephesians, Philippians, Colossians, 1 and 2 Thessalonians, 1 and 2 Timothy, Titus, and Philemon to encourage the believers.

PETER *(Matthew 4; 16–17; Acts 1–15; 1 and 2 Peter)* Peter was Andrew's brother and a fisherman. They were the first of Jesus' twelve apostles. Peter, James, and John were Jesus' closest friends. After Jesus was raised from death and went back to heaven, Peter became one of the leaders of the early church. He wrote two New Testament letters, 1 and 2 Peter. He was killed because of his faith in Jesus.

PHARAOH *(Genesis 12; Exodus 1–15; 1 Chronicles 4; 1 Kings 3–11; 14; 2 Kings 18; 23; Isaiah 36; Jeremiah 44; Ezekiel 29)* Pharaoh was the title Egyptians used for their kings. The pharaoh was commander of their armies, the chief of their courts, the high priest of their religion, and the highest power in the country. There are references to ten pharaohs in the Old Testament.

PHILIP, the apostle (*Matthew 10; John 1; 6; 12; 14*) Philip was one of Jesus' twelve apostles. Philip came from Bethsaida in Galilee and brought Nathanael (Bartholomew) to Jesus.

PHOEBE (*Romans 16*) Phoebe was a lady who was also a servant in the church in the town of Cenchrea. Paul praised her to the church in Rome. He asked them to give her any help she needed because she had been a great help to Paul.

PONTIUS PILATE (*Matthew 27; John 18*) Pontius Pilate was a Roman governor of Judea. Jesus was brought to him for trial. He knew Jesus had not done anything wrong. Pilate allowed him to be crucified anyway because he was afraid of the Jews.

Pontius Pilate Inscription;
Found in Caesarea, the inscription reads "Tiberius (Po)ntius (Pref)ect of Judea", dated 26–36 A.D.

PRISCILLA (*Acts 18; Romans 16; 1 Corinthians 16*) Priscilla and her husband, Aquila, were Jewish Christians. They worked as tentmakers. They traveled with Paul to preach the good news of Jesus. They often let the Christians meet in their house to worship God.

RACHEL (*Genesis 29–31; 33; 35*) Rachel was the younger daughter of Laban. Jacob married her. She was the mother of Joseph and Benjamin.

RAHAB (*Joshua 2; 6; Matthew 1; Hebrews 11; James 2*) Rahab was a woman who lived in Jericho. She hid the Israelite spies because of her faith in God. She also helped them to escape. Because of her faith, she and the people in her house were saved when the Israelites invaded Jericho. She is listed in the family of Jesus as the mother of Boaz.

REBEKAH (*Genesis 22; 24–28*) Rebekah was the wife of Isaac and mother of Jacob and Esau. When Isaac was old, Rebekah helped Jacob trick Isaac into giving him the blessing for the oldest son.

REUBEN (*Genesis 37; 46; Joshua 13*) Reuben was the oldest of Jacob's twelve sons. The other brothers wanted to kill

JeaLous Peas!

Every year on our birthdays, Pa gave us each a pair of mittens. Not very useful to a French Pea living in the desert! But for Little Joe's birthday Pa gave him a beautiful, colorful vest made of the finest calf hide. The brothers and I were very jealous; jealous enough to throw him into an old abandoned mineshaft.

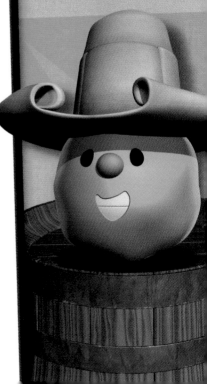

Kind Daughter (in-Law)!

Sweet, Petunia: her eyes are sparkly and her hair is neat. She was named the princess of her senior prom. Now she lives as a peasant with her aging mom (in-law).

Ruth the Moabite;
Illustration from the Dore Bible, published in 1866, England

Joseph because they were jealous of him. Reuben convinced them to put him in a dry well. He planned to come back to let Joseph out. Before he could do that, the brothers sold Joseph as a slave.

RHODA *(Acts 12)* Rhoda was a servant girl in the home of John Mark's mother, Mary. After an angel led Peter out of prison, he went to Mary's house. When he knocked on the door, Rhoda answered. But she was so surprised it was Peter, she forgot to let him in!

RUTH *(book of Ruth)* Ruth showed great love for her mother-in-law, Naomi. After their husbands died, Ruth took care of Naomi. Naomi introduced her to Boaz, who married her. Ruth was David's great-grandmother.

SALOME *(Mark 15–16)* Salome was the wife of Zebedee and mother of James and John, who were apostles of Jesus. She was one of the women who found the tomb empty when they went to put spices on Jesus' body. She also saw Jesus after he came back to life.

SAMSON *(Judges 13–16)* Samson was one of Israel's judges. He was known for his great strength.

Samson made a promise to God not to tell anyone how he got his strength. But he disobeyed and told Delilah it was because of his long hair. The Philistines captured him, cut his hair, and put out his eyes. As his hair grew back, so did his strength. He died by pulling down a huge building, killing many Philistines and himself.

SAMUEL *(1 Samuel 3–16; 19)*
Samuel was the last judge of Israel. Samuel anointed Saul as Israel's first king, and, later, he anointed David.

SARAH *(Genesis 11–12; 16–18; 20–21)* Sarah was Abraham's wife. When she was told at the age of ninety that she would have a son, she laughed. But she did indeed have a son named Isaac.

SATAN *(1 Chronicles 21; Job 1; Matthew 4; Luke 10; Acts 5;*

26) Satan is the name for the devil who is known to be the enemy of both God and man.

SAUL *(1 Samuel 9–31)* Saul was the first king of Israel who turned away from God. He tried to kill David several times. Three of his sons, including Jonathan, died in the battle of Gilboa.

SAUL *(Acts 13)* Saul was the Jewish name for Paul. He changed his name to a Greek name, Paul. He was called the apostle to the Gentiles.

SHADRACH *(Daniel 1; 3)* Shadrach was a good friend of Daniel. He would not bow down and worship a false god. When he and Meshach and Abednego would not obey, King Nebuchadnezzar threw them into a fiery furnace, but God saved them!

Mt. Gilboa;
Site of Saul's battle with the Philistines

You Can Call Me Rack!

Shack and Benny and I were excited when Mr. Nezzer made us junior executives. We got new ties and everything. But when we realized that we would have to bow to his ninety-foot bunny statue, we decided that being junior executives wasn't that important.

SHEM *(Genesis 7; 9–10; 1 Chronicles 1)* Shem was one of Noah's three sons. Shem and his wife were saved in the ark during the Flood. Shem's descendants became the Jews and the other nations who live in that part of the world.

SILAS *(Acts 15–17; 2 Corinthians 1; 1 Thessalonians 1)* Silas was a faithful leader in the Jerusalem church. He was a good friend to Paul and went with Paul on his second missionary trip. They were put into prison together in the city of Philippi.

SIMON *(Matthew 10; Mark 3; Luke 6; Acts 1)* Simon was one of Jesus' twelve apostles. He was also know as the Zealot.

King Solomon;
Hebrew pentateuch, Coburg, 1395

SOLOMON *(1 Kings 1–11)* Solomon was the son of David and Bathsheba. He took his father's place as the king of Israel for forty years. He is known for his riches and wisdom. He built the first temple in Jerusalem.

STEPHEN *(Acts 6–7)* Stephen was a faithful Jew who spoke Greek. He was one of seven men chosen to serve the church in Jerusalem. Stephen became the first person killed for believing in Christ.

THADDAEUS *(Matthew 10; Mark 3)* Thaddaeus was one of Jesus' twelve apostles.

THOMAS *(Matthew 10; Mark 3; John 11; 20–21)* Thomas was one of Jesus' twelve apostles. After Jesus had been raised from death, Thomas needed to see him for himself before he believed it. Because of this, some people call him Doubting Thomas.

TIMOTHY *(Acts 16–17; 1 and 2 Timothy)* Timothy was a young friend and helper of the apostle Paul. Timothy's grandmother Lois and mother Eunice taught him the scriptures. Timothy went on Paul's second missionary trip, and later became a leader in the church in Ephesus. Paul wrote two letters to him.

TITUS *(2 Corinthians 2; 7–8; book of Titus)* Titus was a Gentile friend and companion to Paul. He was on the island of Crete to help the church there. Paul wrote a letter to him.

URIAH *(2 Samuel 11)* Uriah was a soldier in King David's army.

St. Thomas;
Bronze bowl engraved with scenes of the life of St. Thomas, dated 12th century, found in the Church of the Nativity, Bethlehem

He was married to Bathsheba. When David fell in love with her, he sent Uriah into battle so he would be killed.

VASHTI *(Esther 1)* Vashti was King Xerxes' wife and queen of Persia. She made King Xerxes very angry. So, he got a new queen. Esther was Xerxes' queen after Vashti.

XERXES *(book of Esther)* King Xerxes chose Esther, a Jewish girl, as his queen. Xerxes' chief officer, Haman, made a plan to kill all the Jews. Esther had the courage to tell the king about the plan. When the king heard about the plot, he had Haman killed. He brought in Esther's cousin, Mordecai, to take Haman's place.

ZACCHAEUS *(Luke 19)* Zacchaeus was a tax collector. Because he was a small man, he climbed a sycamore tree so he could see Jesus over the crowd. Jesus saw him and went to his home with him. Zacchaeus changed his life and followed Jesus.

ZECHARIAH *(Ezra 5; book of Zechariah)* Zechariah was a priest and prophet during the time of Ezra. Like Haggai, he encouraged the people to obey and serve God by rebuilding the temple.

ZECHARIAH *(Luke 1)* Zechariah was the father of John the Baptist. He was a priest who served at the temple in Jerusalem. When an angel of the Lord told him he and his wife, Elizabeth, would have a son, he wanted to know how he could

be sure. So the angel told him he would not be able to speak until the baby was born. When he wrote on a tablet that the new baby's name was John, he could speak again.

ZEPHANIAH *(book of Zephaniah)* Zephaniah was a prophet during the time of King Josiah in Judah. He wrote the book of Zephaniah. It told of God's punishment to Judah and their enemies. But he ended by saying that God's people would return to Judah.

ZIPPORAH *(Exodus 2; 18)* Zipporah was the wife of Moses. She was from the land of Midian. He met her when he ran away to Midian from Egypt.

Moses and Zipporah meet Aaron on his return to Egypt; Illustration from the Golden Hagada, dated 1320

no TICKLING!

That Haman. He is one sneaky gourd. He tricked me into signing an edict to have Mordecai and his entire family banished to the Island of Perpetual Tickling. I should never have signed that paper without looking at it. Thank goodness my little queenie-poo set me straight!

Living Day By Day!

WHAT KIND OF DESSERTS DID THEY EAT IN THE DESERT?

Hi kids! Welcome to the food section of the VeggieTales Atlapedia. Okay, my brother Jimmy and I are going to tell you all about how the people lived during Bible times, not just about their food. But the food discussions will most certainly be the most interesting! For instance, did you know that a shepherd living in New Testament times never had a pudding cup in his lunch? It's true. There was no sweet reward for eating his bologna sandwich! Life was hard in Bible times. C'mon, we'll show you!

Families

The families in Israel were usually made up of very large households. Aunts, uncles, cousins, grandparents, and even great-grandparents often lived together in a home with a child's brothers, sisters, and parents. If the extended family didn't live together under one roof, they often lived in small homes connected to each other or very close to one another.

The oldest male adult was usually the head of each household. This person determined how his household was run, made all the important decisions, and gave out rules and orders for what should be done on a daily basis. It was very unusual for a man to move away from his family.

Wealthier families employed servants. These servants were considered a part of the overall household too.

Marriages were handled much differently than they are today. A child's parents made all the arrangements for a marriage. When a boy turned thirteen years old, he was old enough to get engaged. This was also called being "betrothed." A girl could become engaged once she reached the age of twelve.

A boy's father would visit a girl's parents and make a marriage proposal. He would offer a dowry to the girl's family, because he would be taking one of the family's workers. (A dowry was a gift given by the boy's father to the family of the girl he was going to marry.) Each worker was considered to be very valuable! The dowry that was offered could be anything from a certain amount of money, to one or more animals, a piece of land, or even goods like food or clothing. When the bride's family accepted the groom's gift, a contract would be drawn up, signed, and witnessed.

The parents would set a date for the marriage, often a year or more after the arrangements were made. Invitations would go out to family and friends, and the bride's dress would be made. The young man and woman rarely

Wedding ring;
Ancient traditional Jewish wedding ring from Central Europe.
The shape of a house symbolizes a prosperous family life.

We are Family!

My mommy always tells me to do what's right. To wash behind my ears and try to be polite. You see she loves me so. That's why she tells me what I need to know!

Make Your Own Pottery!

Pottery served a number of different purposes during Bible times. It was molded to create a variety of utensils, containers, and ornate items. The clay was warmed in the hot sun and then stomped on to make it soft. Then the clay was molded into an object on a flat surface or by using a potter's wheel. Pottery was dried in the sun to harden.

You will need air-drying clay (which you can get at a craft store), plastic table coverings, tempera paints, brushes, water, plastic knives, and cleanup tools.

Begin by deciding what type of pottery you would like to make: a bowl, a vase, a pitcher, and so on. Take the clay and shape it as desired. Try to create an even thickness and take care not to leave any area too thin so that it does not break easily. Smooth the outer surface and use a plastic knife to carve any lines or designs, as desired. Let it dry thoroughly. (Follow drying instructions on the package. Some clays will dry overnight, while others take up to a full week.)

After your pottery has completely dried and hardened, paint as desired.

saw each other before the wedding, but they could send each other notes or gifts.

On the day of the wedding, the groom, his family, and his friends would travel to see the bride as she prepared for the big occasion. When the groom arrived, she would be surrounded by her bridesmaids. A torchlight parade would form as they would travel to the home of the groom. Upon their arrival, the wedding ceremony would take place and then there would be a big celebration that would last for days or even a whole week!

Men and women had very different duties during Bible times. As the head of their families, men were expected to provide for their well-being. A man was to give spiritual guidance and provide for his family's housing and food; he was also responsible for the protection of his family.

It was the woman's job to take care of the house while the man worked outside the home. Women were to care for the children, cook, clean, sew, create pottery, garden or work in the field, shop, and even sell cloth or clothing that she had woven or sewn.

In Proverbs, the Bible describes a good wife like this:

She is worth far more than rubies. Her husband has full confidence in her. . . . She selects wool and flax and works with eager hands . . . she provides food for her family and portions for her servant girls. She considers a field and buys it; out of her earnings she plants a vineyard. . . . She opens her arms to the poor and extends her hands to the needy. . . . All of [her family] are clothed in scarlet. . . . She makes linen garments and sells them.
Proverbs 31:10–11; 13; 15–16; 20; 24

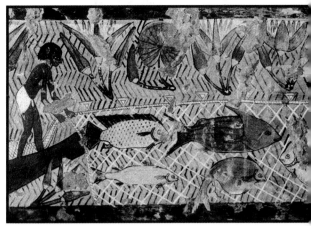

Fishing on the Nile;
Wall painting from Thebes, tomb of Ramsses II, 1292–1255 B.C.

Babies traveled everywhere with their mothers. A child was wrapped snuggly with strips of cloth to make a tight bundle, making it easy for the child to be carried on the mother's back as she worked. At night, a mother would unwrap her baby, take off her own cloak, and hang it from a beam or two sticks to form a hammock.

A child was named in a special ceremony on the eighth day after the baby's birth. The name given to the child always had a special meaning.

Girls grew up and learned how to run a household from their mother. They were taught to cook, clean, sew, garden, do small home repairs, and do any chores that were helpful to her mother. Girls were educated in the home by parents and grandparents, because they were rarely allowed to go to school.

Boys usually grew up to learn the same profession as their father. At home, they were often required to do difficult chores such as farming, animal care, and protecting the family. Boys were allowed to go to synagogue school when they turned six years of age. They learned things like history, geography, law, and literature. They only had one textbook for all their classes — the Jewish scriptures. Boys who showed great promise were sent to study with a rabbi and learn his teachings. At age twelve, a boy received his "Bar Mitzvah," which was a special ceremony that showed he had become a man.

OCCUPATIONS

Men had a number of different occupations to choose from in Bible times. Some of them included being a: fisherman, farmer, shepherd, doctor, craftsman, carpenter, tax collector, tailor, baker, money changer, jewelry maker, weaver, miner, scribe, or priest. People also made many things with their own hands—like tents, sandals, bricks, fabric, and glass.

Farming was one of the main occupations during Bible times. Farmers grew fruits such as grapes and figs, olives, and grains like barley and wheat.

Fishermen spent long hours making large nets to cast into the water either from the land or to stretch between two boats that would then drag the net through the water and onto the shore to fish.

Doctors didn't have hospitals to practice in like we have today. They went to people's homes to treat them. Larger towns were often fortunate enough to have a surgeon too. One of the temple officials was usually a doctor who had the job of taking care of the temple priest. The Gospel writer Luke was a trained physician.

Make Your Own Fishing Net!

(Adult help needed with this project.)

A net was an essential tool for fishermen during Bible times.

You will need to make a wooden loom by hammering together four 12" x 1" x 1/4" strips of wood to create a square frame. Measure and mark out seven evenly spaced dots on each of the four opposite sides of the frame. Hammer in 1" nails into each dot, leaving half of the nail exposed.

To create a fisherman's net, you will need fourteen pieces of sturdy string. Attach seven of the strings pulled tight between two sets of nails opposite each other on the loom, tying a simple knot at each start and end. Next, attach the second set of seven strings to the remaining set of nails. Tie a simple knot at each start and an "overhand knot" at each intersecting string on the loom. Try to maintain equal spacing between each set of strings.

Pull the net off the loom. Then take a final piece of string and thread it between the loops of each string at one end of the net to create the top. Take four small corks and very carefully slit them one-third of the way through, lengthwise. Slide the top string through each of the cork slits, spacing them evenly apart. The net will now float in the water!

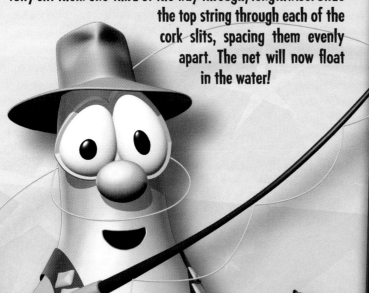

Carpenters made furniture, chariots, carts, doors, panels, beams, ladders, tools, and even the crosses used for crucifixions. A carpenter's tools included many things carpenters use today such as a hammer, drill, plumb line, awl, chisel, set-square, and a saw.

Potters molded various pots, bowls, oil-lamps, and vases out of clay. Pottery was molded by hand or created from a wheel that spun around. After a piece was completed, it was heated in an oven called a kiln to make the clay hard. After it hardened, it was often painted in bright colors.

Potter's wheel;
Stone potter's wheel found in Judea,
dating from the Israelite period

Shepherds cared for and protected their flocks of sheep. They often had to travel great distances to find fresh grass for the sheep to eat. It was the shepherd's job to count the sheep every night and watch out for wild animals that might attack.

Rural house;
Reconstruction of a 4th-century A.D. house in Northern Israel

BiBLe-Time Homes

Tents were used by some people as a permanent home. Some people traveled with their tent homes and some families stayed in one place for long stretches of time, living in a tent.

Small homes were constructed from sun-baked bricks for most families during Bible times. There was no need for many rooms because so many activities took place out of doors. The rooms were kept dark to keep things cool in the hot sun.

Poor people lived in one-room homes that they had to share even with their animals. A raised platform at one end of the room was built for people to sleep on. Floors were simply dried mud. Windows were high and small.

Most homes had flat roofs. Because the homes were built close together, people could often walk from rooftop to rooftop. Rooftops were also used as extra space for people to go so they could visit, pray, or dry laundry, figs, linen, or fruits. A ladder or staircase alongside the outer wall of the home was constructed to get up to the roof. A roof often leaked, and people would keep mud and leaves to fix the roof.

Rural house interior;
Reconstruction of a 4th-century A.D. house interior

Make Your Own Mosaic!

Mosaics were used for a variety of Bible-time decorations and art. They were not only used to decorate the insides of buildings, but also outdoor walkways and courtyards. They were used by both Egyptians and the Greeks. Mosaics were constructed out of various materials that included metals, bricks, stones, pebbles, and even jewels.

You will need poster board or cardboard squares, cotton-tipped swabs, glue, pencils, and multicolored, dried beans, peas, pebbles, cereals, or other small items.

Decide what type of mosaic design you wish to make (such as the symbol of a fish or a cross). Draw your design onto the cardboard with pencil. Next, choose the type of items you would like to use to create the mosaic. You will need at least two contrasting colors, one for the design and one for the background.

Use a cotton-tipped swab to spread glue onto a small area of the mosaic design drawn on the cardboard. Then place the items chosen to illustrate that design (such as dried green peas). When the illustrated design is completely covered, then begin to spread glue on the remainder of the cardboard (working with small areas at a time). Use the other contrasting colored item to cover that area (such as light brown dried beans). Cover the entire board. Dry thoroughly.

The interiors of homes were very simply decorated. Not much furniture was needed. Homes were lit with small oil lamps. The doors of homes were very low, and people often had to bend over to enter.

Families with money often had two-story homes with several rooms. The ground floor was often used to store items, cook food, or house animals. Sometimes, courtyards were created around the house to hold the family's animals.

House interior;
Reconstruction of a rich house in upper Jerusalem

Some very wealthy people often had homes made from stone instead of sun-baked clay bricks. It was a sign of great wealth if someone had a room of his or her own. The rich had beautiful rugs, wall hangings, mosaics, pottery, and furniture pieces.

Grain pits were used to store large amounts of food supplies. Villages had large pits that were dug in the ground for this purpose.

Hebrew and Greek cities were often built with high walls that could protect people from their enemies. A gateway was made in the wall to enter and exit. This was the only way into the city. Large towers were constructed for use in defense.

Inside the gate, people would gather to buy and sell their goods. This was also a place where men could come and look for work.

People got their water through wells. Women and children went to a village well that was shared by the entire community. Some villages also had a cistern to collect the water. A cistern was a pear-shaped pit that was lined at the bottom with plaster so it would not leak. Some houses had cisterns beneath them that held rainwater that ran off of the roof.

People in Bible times rarely had bathtubs and there were no showers. Because water was scarce, people were unable to wash their entire bodies very often. Foot washing, however, was a common practice. The land got very little rain, and because people traveled mostly by foot, their feet would get dusty and dirty. Sometimes the people used the ashes of burnt plants as soap. Then they rubbed olive oil onto their skin to keep it from getting too dry. Others bathed in rivers.

The wealthy people used perfume and makeup such as rouge, lipstick, and nail polish.

Hair was worn long by both men and women during Old Testament times. Men often had long beards. In the New Testament times, men began to copy the Roman styles and began to have shorter hair and no beards. Women often wore their hair loose or in braids wrapped on top of their head.

Village well;
Reconstruction scene of a village well

FOOT WASHING!

It was just before the Passover Feast, and Jesus knew that the time had come for him to leave this world and go back to his Father. Jesus loved his disciples very much so he wanted to share this last meal with them. Because they traveled by foot, their feet were very dusty and dirty. It felt good to have them cleaned and refreshed with cool water at the end of the day.

Jesus wanted to show his disciples the importance of being a servant to others, so he chose to wash their feet.

You will need a wide bowl or basin, some warm water, a wash cloth, and a towel. Invite someone to remove their shoes and socks as you kneel before them with the basin and towels. Gently take their foot and dip it into the warm water and wash it with the cloth. Dry it with the towel and do the other one. Remind those whose feet you wash that it is a joy to be a servant to them!

Make Your Own Matzo Bread!

(Adult supervision needed.)

Preheat oven to 375 degrees. Combine in a bowl: 1 tsp. salt and 1/2 tsp. baking soda. Add 2 tablespoons of butter and 2/3 cup buttermilk. Stir dough into a ball and knead for a few strokes. Divide dough into several pieces and roll out very thin on a floured board. Lay sheet of dough on ungreased flat baking pans. Prick with a fork. Cut into 4-inch squares with a sharp knife or pizza cutter. Bake 10-12 minutes or until lightly browned.

This easy unleavened bread will turn out very much like soda crackers.

Table arrangement;
Model of a Roman period table arrangement

FOOD AND MEALS

Cooking equipment in Bible times was very simple. Those who had to cook outside used a small ring of stones placed in a circle, and a fire was built on the inside of the ring. Pots were balanced on the stones or placed directly inside the stones among the flames. Nicer homes had ovens made out of pottery or small mud bricks. A fire was lit at the bottom, making the walls very hot. Breads and other foods were cooked directly on top of the hot surface, much like we use a griddle today.

By New Testament times, most homes had stoves with fires within for cooking. Even corn could be popped by placing ears of corn on a large baking sheet. Kids probably had great fun "catching" their treat as the corn was popped into the air! New meat was roasted over open fires, but was also a luxury that was saved for special occasions. Meat was not eaten every day. Fish was much more common than meat at daily meals. God had special rules for what the

Clay oven;
Used for home cooking by placing the pot on the opening on the top

Israelites could eat and cook. For example, meat could never be cooked or mixed with milk. Pork was considered "unclean" and not allowed to be eaten.

The most common grains for bread were wheat and barley. As bread was made almost every day, people would grind just enough grain for that day's needs. Sweet bread was made by adding a little honey to the recipe.

Grindstone mills were created, and people or animals were hitched to a wooden frame that turned the grindstones.

Goat's milk was very common in many recipes. When it was left in a bowl overnight, the air would sour it and yogurt was the result. If it was left even longer, then curds and whey were created. The curds could be mixed with salt to make cheese.

People grew their own herbs and vegetables. There was often a good variety of fruit and vegetables for most people to eat on a daily basis. Some families had a "fatted calf," which they kept indoors and fed well. It was kept for a very special occasion when it would be killed and cooked.

Grapes were squeezed to extract the juice. One way of squeezing them was to stomp on them in a winepress. The juice ran down channels and was collected and put into wineskins to ferment and to produce wine.

Grinding mill;
A grinding mill consisting of two conical stones which break the grains when turned around each other

make Your Own Tie-Dye!

You will need newspaper, white cotton squares or T-shirts, a large pot that is not aluminum, a large spoon, purple fabric dye, rubber bands, hot water, tongs, latex gloves, clothespins, and a clothesline.

Use rubber bands to section off parts of a white cloth or T-shirt. Follow the dye directions on the package. After dyeing, use tongs to lift the cloth out of the hot pot of water and rinse in cold water. Take the rubber bands off and rinse again. Squeeze out the cloth and hang dry.

Olives were squeezed to obtain olive oil. Some olive presses used donkeys to roll two heavy stones over the fruit to make the oily juice run out.

The only sweetener in Bible times was honey. It was collected from bee hives. Proverbs 25:16 advised people to not eat too much honey as it could make them sick!

Two meals were prepared each day, except for Sunday. Lunches were created from flat bread, olives, raisins, dried figs, and cheese. Dinners were often large pots of vegetable stew and bread that was dipped in the stew. Stews used ingredients such as lentils, water, salt, herbs, garlic, leeks, onions, carrots, and potatoes. Because no fires could be lit on the Sabbath, the people ate leftovers on that day.

Wealthier families could also afford imported foods, including rare spices such as cinnamon.

CLOTHiNG

Women made fabric using a spinning wheel or by weaving material on a loom. They made clothing for their family and often made extra to sell in the marketplace.

Sheep's wool was the material most commonly used for making clothes. Flax was grown to provide fibers for linen, which was soft and strong. The hair from camels and goats could be spun into thread and woven into a rough, heavy cloth suitable for rough outerwear and for tents.

Sheep were sheared once a year to provide wool. This was a very fun and festive occasion. Natural wools came in various browns and whites. Wool was washed and dyed to different colors. Purple was an

Jewelry;
Excavated in Dear-el Balach, south of Gaza, 14th century B.C.

High priest garments;
Drawn according to Numbers 27:21, including the breast plate (ephod) consisting of twelve precious stones symbolizing the twelve tribes of Isreal

especially expensive dye. The wool was also combed, spun, and woven.

A variety of patterns and colors could be woven into cloth. Stripes and checks were easy to make. Skillful weavers could create much fancier patterns. Other cloths were embroidered.

People wore long, flowing robes, called mantles. Women's mantles were more elaborate and colorful than men's. Women usually wore two tunics, one inner one (like undergarments) and an outer, longer one that would normally be tied at the waist. The mantle was an almost square piece of cloth, similar to a blanket. In nice weather, this was generally worn around the shoulders as a cloak.

The rich had brightly dyed clothing. Many times, a person's clothing identified his profession.

Most people had a simple pair of sandals to wear for travel. Simple sandals consisted of a cloth, wood, grass, or cowhide sole fastened to the ankle by a leather thong that passed between the large and second toe. Wealthier people sometimes wore all-leather slippers.

Turbans were created for people to wear on their heads to protect them from the sun. If a turban was not available, a piece of square cloth was held to the head by a simple cord.

Long coats called cloaks were worn over the clothes because it was often chilly at night, even though the days were most often quite hot. The poor wrapped themselves up in this garment at night. The poor had cloaks of camel hair or goatskin, but most had cloaks made of wool.

In the Old Testament, God's law said that men were to wear tassels on the four corners of their cloaks, as a reminder of God's commands (*Numbers 15:39*). Later, these tassels were attached to a square woolen cloth worn under the cloak. Jesus criticized the religious teachers of the time for wearing extra long tassels just for show.

Precious stones, shells, ivory, silver, and gold were all used to make jewelry, including rings, earrings, nose rings, pendants, necklaces, and bracelets.

WORSHIP

The Sabbath was the seventh, or last, day of the week; a day set aside by God as a day of rest, remembrance, and worship for God. When the Jews were taken into exile and could no longer travel to the temple, they set up the synagogue so that they could continue to learn about and pray to God. It was a very busy place, used for worship, educational, and social activities.

Synagogue means "congregation" or "gathering place." Synagogues were an important place of worship and learning.

Some synagogues were very elaborate, while others were simpler. One of the primary elements of a synagogue was the ark, which contained the sacred scroll of the Torah. The ark was always elevated and placed at a focal point in the synagogue. Other elements were menorahs, which were large lamps that burned continuously,

Nazareth, Church-Synagogue;
Believed to be the place where Jesus preached on the Sabbath

Ark with Torah;
Decorated ark with Torah scrolls, Jerusalem

and a pulpit from which the Torah was read and Scripture was taught. Male and female worshipers did not sit together, and there was a separate section for lepers.

Jewish men covered their heads when entering the synagogue. These head coverings were called yarmulkes or kippas.

The rabbi was the spiritual leader and the most holy of the Jews. He was a teacher and preacher of religion and was often the one to hold and read from the sacred Torah during worship. The Torah was a large scroll containing the first five books of the Bible, also known as the Pentateuch or the Law of Moses.

Make Your Own Prayer Shawl!

The Jewish people wore shawls called a tallith. The prayer shawl was worn by male worshipers as a reminder to observe all of God's laws. It was worn during the daytime worship and sometimes during funeral services.

You will need a variety of cotton and felt fabric, scissors, rulers, measuring tape, fabric paint, and yarn to match the fabric.

Select a piece of fabric and cut a long, narrow length three to four feet and approximately six inches wide. Create fringes at each end of the shawl in one of two ways. One way is to cut a one-inch slit every one-half inch all along the edge. The second way is to cut a small hole every one-half inch apart at each edge of the shawl. Then cut three six-inch strands of yarn for each hole. Take the three strands and pull them halfway through a hole and knot in place. Repeat for each hole.

Use fabric paint to decorate the tallith with symbols or a colorful striping in the last five to eight inches of each end (right before the fringe).

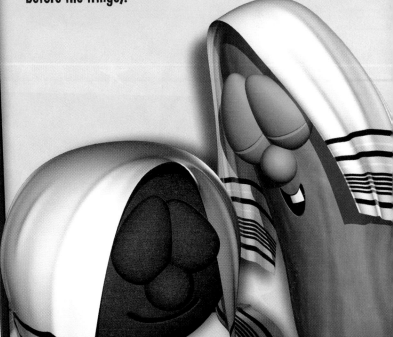

Make Your Own Shema Scroll!

The Shema is a creed or prayer. It was recited at the beginning of synagogue worship as a way to reinforce the importance of remembering God's commands. There are three passages in the Shema:
(1) Deuteronomy 6:4–9
(2) Deuteronomy 11:13–21
(3) Numbers 15:37–41

You will need rolled paper or 8 1/2" x 14" paper, thick wooden dowels cut to 14" in length, Bibles, tape, pens, wood glue, small rounded cabinet knobs, and yarn.

Begin by gluing a wooden cabinet knob onto each end of the wooden dowels. Let dry while creating the rest of the scroll. Next, take the rolled paper or 8 1/2" x 14" paper and make it look like authentic papyrus paper used in Bible times by carefully tearing off all of the edges of the paper. When done, carefully crumple up the paper tightly and then unfold it again, smoothing it out as best you can.

Copy one or all of the Shema verses onto the paper. Then tape each end of the paper to one of the wooden dowels and roll each end inward. Tie together with a piece of yarn.

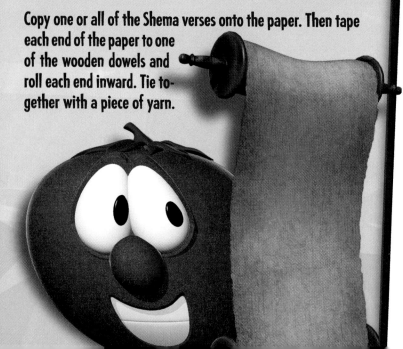

FESTIVALS

God's people held special feasts and festivals throughout the year to remember how much God loved them and cared for them.

• **Sabbath:** God tells his people to do their work in six days, but the seventh day of each week is a day of rest called the Sabbath. Believers are to devote the Sabbath to worship God (Exodus 20:8–11; Leviticus 23:3).

• **Passover** was also known as the Feast of Unleavened Bread. The first Passover took place before the great escape out of Egypt. When Pharoah would not let the people go as Moses requested, God sent plaques to Egypt. The last plaque God created caused the death of the firstborn male in every house that did not believe in him. To avoid this plague, the Israelite households were told to sacrifice a lamb. The meat was to be cooked and eaten; the blood of the lamb was to be spread on the doorposts so that the Lord (see Exodus 12:12–13; 23) would see the display of faith and would pass over the house. The Israelites were told to be ready to leave quickly. They were to dress for travel and make unleavened bread to eat.

• **Feast of Weeks** (also called Pentecost and the Feast of

The Cenacle;
Believed to be the site where Jesus partook in the Passover feast with his disciples (The Last Supper)

Harvest) was held fifty days after the first sheaf of barley was offered to God at the Feast of Unleavened Bread. It was a reminder to the people that they should always offer God the first and best of what they had (Leviticus 23:9–14).

• **Yom Kippur—the Day of Atonement:** On the tenth day of the seventh month, everyone took part in a ceremony to ask God's forgiveness for all that they had done wrong. The high priest offered sacrifices and went into the "holy of holies"—the innermost part of the tabernacle or temple—to present a sacrifice to God. He took two goats, sacrificed one and laid hands on the other's head, confessed the people's wrongdoing, and sent the goat into the desert. It was a way of acting out the belief that God was taking away the people's sins. No work could be performed on this day. Adults could not even eat or drink anything (including water.) They fasted for twenty-five hours beginning right before sunset on the evening before Yom Kippur and ending after nightfall on the day itself (Leviticus 23:26–32).

• **Rosh Hashanah:** In Hebrew, Rosh Hashanah means "head of the year" or "first of the year." Rosh Hashanah is commonly known as the Jewish New Year. The Jewish New Year is a time for looking back at the mistakes of the past year and plan the changes to make in the new year. The name "Rosh Hashanah" is not used in the Bible. The Bible refers to the holiday as the Feast of Trumpet. The holiday is mentioned in Leviticus 23:24–25. People are to have a day of rest. Then people worship God and offer sacrifices. One of the most important observances of this holiday is hearing the sounding of the shofar in the synagogue. The shofar is blown somewhat like a trumpet (Leviticus 23:24–25).

• **Festival of the Booths** (also called the Feast of Tabernacles): This was the most popular and joyful festival, which came at the time of year when the autumn harvest was celebrated. Families remembered when their people had lived as nomads in the desert as they traveled from Egypt to Canaan, and how much God cared for them. When they traveled, they lived temporarily in "booths" made of palm or willow trees. They said prayers and held special ceremonies for the vital winter rain (Leviticus 23:33–43).

FUNERALS

It's a sad time when someone dies. In Jesus' time, when someone died, they wrapped the body in strips of linen along with spices and perfumes. Coffins were not used. People followed a body to be buried. They would be wailing, wearing sackcloth, throwing ashes on themselves, and tearing their clothes as a sign of grief.

The family grave was either a cave or a tomb cut out of the rock. The body was placed inside and the tomb closed with a large stone.

FUN AND GAMES

Children played in a variety of ways during Bible times. Some of those ways are very similar to the ways children play today—others are quite different!

Children have always had imaginations, played dress-up, and imitated weddings and battles. They practiced shooting with homemade bows and arrows and with slingshots and stones. They also had toys. Archaeologists have found game boards of ivory, with playing pieces of stone and clay. Other game boards were scratched on paving stones. Younger children probably enjoyed carved pull toys, dolls, and puppets. Children also played games with dice, balls, spinning tops, rattles, kites, and whistles. They had tossing contests and races. Simple musical instruments could easily be made at home, and children would have time to practice their skills when they were out watching the flocks. David, the shepherd boy who became a king, played a homemade harp while he watched over the flocks.

Burial procession;
Reenactment of a burial
procession as it was performed in a
Jewish community in Roman Jerusalem

Game pieces;
Dice and other game pieces made from bone,
excavated in Tel Mirsim, 15th century B.C.

Children told stories, jokes, and riddles and acted in made-up dramas. People told stories for purposes of entertainment and as a way of passing on stories to generation after generation. Stories can be understood in many different ways. Jesus often told stories called parables that had hidden meanings to help people learn about God in ways they could remember them.

Throughout Bible times, it is clear that many different people enjoyed a variety of sports. The Egyptians, Mesopotamians, Greeks, and Romans enjoyed sports. However, some Jewish people felt they were wrong when the games were performed to honor other gods.

Make Your Own Dreidel!

The dreidel was a game played by the Jewish children. It was created in remembrance of the rededication of the temple. Each letter on the dreidel represents the first letter from a different word in the phrase: Nes gadol hayah sham, which means: a great miracle happened there.

You will need a one-inch wooden cube predrilled with a hole through the center of it, wooden dowels (the same width as the center holed drilled through the cube) 2 1/2" long, glue, permanent markers, and a pencil sharpener.

Write the letters: N, G, H, and S, one on each side of the cube. Sharpen one end of the dowel rod with a pencil sharpener. Place a small amount of glue in each opening of the cube's hole, and then slide the dowel rod through it.

Give each player ten popcorn kernels to start. Players place five of their kernels in the center of the play area. This is called "the pot." Each player takes a turn spinning the dreidel. Players follow the directions for each letter of the dreidel and continue play as long as desired, or until one player has won all of the popcorn kernels.

Letter directions:

N = Do Nothing
G = Take all of the pot
H = Take half of the pot
S = Add one to the pot

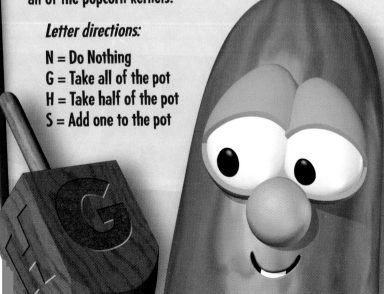

SECTiON 6
THey WenT THaTa Way!

We Do SomeTHinG, SomeTimes!

Hi kids! Pirate Lunt here; along with Larry the Cucumber and Pa Grape. As you know, we're the Pirates Who Don't Do Anything. Although this time we agreed to do something... only because this VeggieTales Atlapedia was in desperate need of our expert advice. Maps! We're pirates... we're very good at maps! And these maps are filled with valuable treasures. Oh, maybe not gold dubloons or even cheese curls. No, these maps will help us to understand our faith in God. Now, that's what I call an invaluable treasure!

BiBLe LaNDS

Most of the Bible events took place in the Holy Land, which is east of the Mediterranean Sea and is now called the Middle East. The region extends from Egypt, where Moses was drawn from the Nile River, to Bethlehem, the birthplace of Jesus, to Mesopotamia (now Iraq) where Abraham was born. The modern countries of Israel, Syria, Jordan, and Lebanon make up this small but important area of world history.

Rome was the capital of government in New Testament times.

Rome

ITALY

Adriatic Sea

BULGARIA

ALBANIA

MACEDONIA

Thessalonica

Berea

Letter written to the church of Thessalonica.

GREECE

Aegean Sea

Rhegium

Athens

SICILY

Corinth

Ephe

Syracuse

Letter written to the church of Corinth.

CRETE

Malta Malts;
While searching for Samson's hairbrush, Minnesota Cuke stopped in Malta for a Malt.

LIBYA

Judean Desert - Because of its lack of water and passable routes, the Judean Desert has been mostly uninhabited throughout history. It was a great place for seeking refuge from enemies. When David was hiding from King Saul, he hid in various places in the Judean wilderness. John the Baptist preached here, and most likely this was where Jesus was tempted. Herod the Great built two fortresses in this area for protection in case his people ever revolted against him.

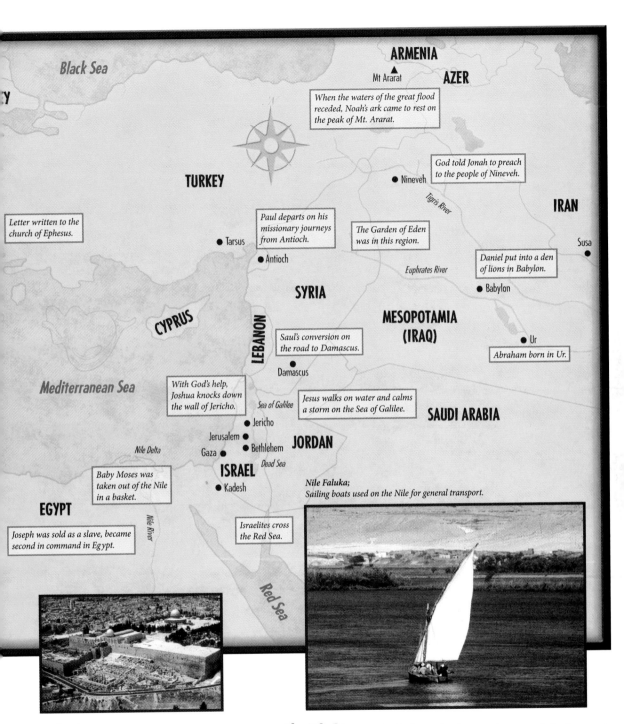

ARMENIA

Mt Ararat ▲

AZER

When the waters of the great flood receded, Noah's ark came to rest on the peak of Mt. Ararat.

Black Sea

God told Jonah to preach to the people of Nineveh.

• Nineveh

Tigris River

IRAN

TURKEY

Letter written to the church of Ephesus.

Paul departs on his missionary journeys from Antioch.

The Garden of Eden was in this region.

• Tarsus

• Antioch

Euphrates River

Susa •

Daniel put into a den of lions in Babylon.

SYRIA

• Babylon

CYPRUS

LEBANON

MESOPOTAMIA (IRAQ)

• Ur

Saul's conversion on the road to Damascus.

Abraham born in Ur.

Mediterranean Sea

•
Damascus

With God's help, Joshua knocks down the wall of Jericho.

Sea of Galilee

Jesus walks on water and calms a storm on the Sea of Galilee.

SAUDI ARABIA

• Jericho

Jerusalem •

Nile Delta

• Bethlehem

JORDAN

Gaza •

Dead Sea

Baby Moses was taken out of the Nile in a basket.

ISRAEL

• Kadesh

Nile Faluka;
Sailing boats used on the Nile for general transport.

EGYPT

Nile River

Joseph was sold as a slave, became second in command in Egypt.

Israelites cross the Red Sea.

Red Sea

Temple Mount – At the center of Jerusalem was the sacred Jewish temple. Now, only the western or Wailing Wall of the temple remains.

The Nile River - The father of African rivers and the longest river in the world. It rises south of the equator and flows northward through northeastern Africa to drain into the Mediterranean Sea. It has a length of about 4,132 miles and drains into an area estimated at 1,293,000 square miles.

exodus

The nation of Israel — Jacob's descendants — lived a good life in the land of Goshen, beside the Nile River in Egypt, until the Egyptians took the Israelites as slaves. God sent Moses to rescue them. Moses demanded, "Let my people go!" but Pharaoh refused. Only after ten dreadful plagues did Pharaoh give in, but then he changed his mind again! This time he sent his army to chase after the Israelites, but God parted the Red Sea, allowing Moses and the Israelites to cross safely. From there they traveled south to Mount Sinai, where God gave Moses the Ten Commandments. Then they wandered the Sinai Desert for fourty years until finally reaching the Promised Land.

Pyramid – The Israelite slaves were forced to make bricks made from clay and straw but still managed to build great buildings such as the Sagara Pyramid.

Saqara Pyramid;
The tomb of King Djoser of the 3rd Dynasty, it is the oldest of the pyramids dating from years 2686-2613 B.C.

Saving Her Brother;
Miriam hides her baby brother, Moses, in the waters of the Nile. He is found by the Pharaoh's daughter and raised as an Egyptian, but ends up leading the Israelites out of Egypt.

Nile River

- · *Traditional Route of the Exodus*

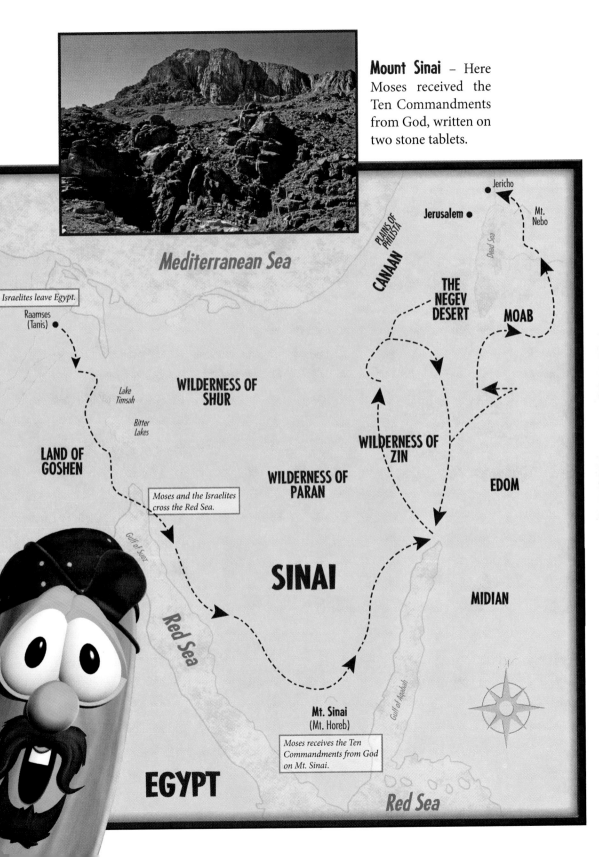

Mount Sinai – Here Moses received the Ten Commandments from God, written on two stone tablets.

Mediterranean Sea

Israelites leave Egypt.
Raamses (Tanis)

PLAINS OF PHILSTA

Jerusalem

Jericho

Mt. Nebo

Dead Sea

CANAAN

THE NEGEV DESERT

MOAB

Lake Timsah

WILDERNESS OF SHUR

Bitter Lakes

LAND OF GOSHEN

Moses and the Israelites cross the Red Sea.

WILDERNESS OF PARAN

WILDERNESS OF ZIN

EDOM

Nile River

Gulf of Suez

SINAI

MIDIAN

Red Sea

Mt. Sinai (Mt. Horeb)

Gulf of Aqabah

Moses receives the Ten Commandments from God on Mt. Sinai.

EGYPT

Red Sea

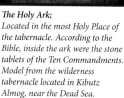

The Holy Ark;
Located in the most Holy Place of the tabernacle. According to the Bible, inside the ark were the stone tablets of the Ten Commandments. Model from the wilderness tabernacle located in Kibutz Almog, near the Dead Sea.

TABERNACLE

The Israelites built the tabernacle during the Exodus. Since they were traveling to the Promised Land, they needed an easy-to-move place of worship that they could take with them. The tabernacle was a tent draped with colorful curtains made of goat's hair and a roof made of male sheep skins. Inside, it was divided into two areas separated by a curtain.

The outer room contained a large candle-holder, the seven-branched candelabrum; the inner room — also known as the "holy of holies" — contained the ark of the covenant.

Tiberias Mosaic;
Detail of a mosaic floor depicting the holy ark surrounded by two large candelabras and other ceremonial objects. Hamat Tiberias, 4-5th century A.D.

SOLOMON'S TEMPLE

Solomon became king of Israel when his father, King David, died around 970 B.C. Solomon was very wealthy and very wise. He built a beautiful temple in Jerusalem that became Israel's permanent house of worship. In front of the temple stood two huge pillars made of bronze. Inside the doors was a chamber called the Holy Place. Its walls were covered with cedar paneling, decorated with gold flowers. There was an inner sanctuary called the holy of holies. Huge winged angels, or cherubims, sat beside the ark of the covenant, which held the Ten Commandments. Sacrifices were offered morning and evening at the great altar.

Solomon's Temple;
Reconstruction drawing of Solomon's
temple built in the 9th century B.C.

Jesus' Birth, Ministry, and Travels

Tiberias – An aerial view of the city and the Sea of Galilee.

In the first century B.C., the Holy Land became part of the Roman Empire. King Herod had to pay taxes to Augustus, so he ordered everyone to return to their family homes to be registered. This is why Mary and Joseph traveled to the town of Bethleham. Once they got to Bethlehem, baby Jesus was born.

Jesus grew up in Nazareth and worked as a carpenter, helping his father. As a boy he studied in the temple, amazing the religious leaders with his knowledge. Around the age of thirty, Jesus was baptized by John the Baptist, and God's Holy Spirit came down in the form of a dove, while a voice from heaven said, "You are my beloved Son; in you I am well pleased." This event began Jesus' ministry. He traveled around Galilee with his disciples, teaching and preaching and performing many miracles.

Torah Scroll – During Jewish services in synagogues, the Torah, or Hebrew Bible, is read. Jesus would have read from the scroll when he was in the synagogue.

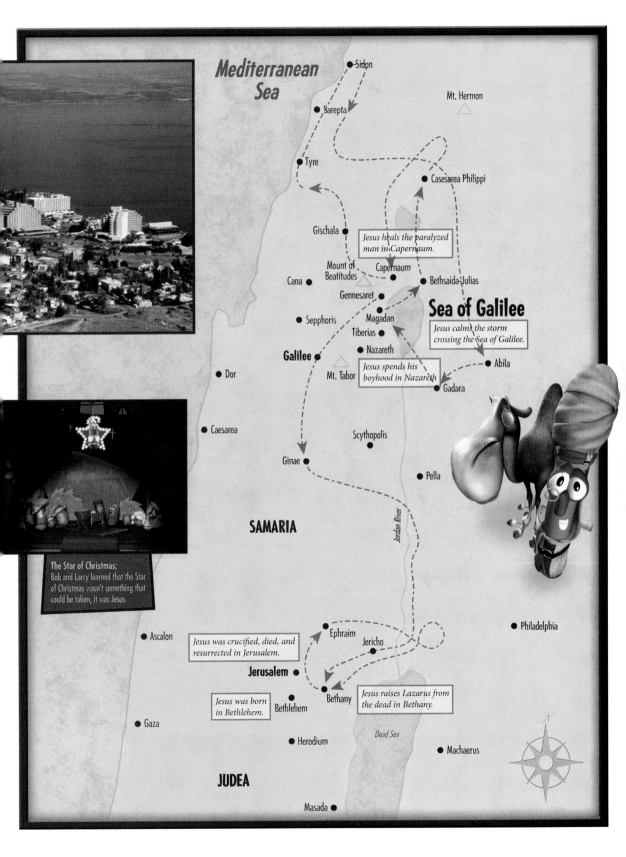

Mediterranean Sea

Sidon

Mt. Hermon △

Sarepta

Tyre

Casesarea Philippi

Gischala

Jesus heals the paralyzed man in Capernaum.

Mount of Beatitudes

Cana

Capernaum

Bethsaida-Julias

Sea of Galilee

Gennesaret

Sepphoris

Magadan

Tiberias

Jesus calms the storm crossing the Sea of Galilee.

Nazareth

Galilee

Mt. Tabor

Jesus spends his boyhood in Nazareth

Abila

Gadara

Dor

Caesarea

Scythopolis

Pella

Ginae

SAMARIA

Jordan River

The Star of Christmas; Bob and Larry learned that the Star of Christmas wasn't something that could be taken, it was Jesus.

Philadelphia

Ascalon

Ephraim

Jericho

Jesus was crucified, died, and resurrected in Jerusalem.

Jerusalem

Bethany

Jesus was born in Bethlehem.

Bethlehem

Jesus raises Lazarus from the dead in Bethany.

Gaza

Herodium

Dead Sea

Machaerus

JUDEA

Masada

PAUL'S MISSIONARY JOURNEYS

A man named Saul did not believe that Jesus had risen from the dead, so he began persecuting the Jews. But during a journey from Jerusalem to Damascus, a bright light suddenly appeared and blinded Saul, and he heard a voice saying, "Saul, Saul, why are you persecuting me?" Saul became a Christian, he repented his sins, God changed his name to Paul, and he became one of the greatest missionaries of the Christian church. He traveled to many cities spreading the gospel of Jesus Christ.

CORSICA

SARDINIA

Adriatic Sea

Paul wrote many letters, including letters to the Romans.

● Rome

● Naples

ITALY

SICILY

● Tunis

TUNISIA

● Paul's First Journey

● Paul's Second Journey

● Paul's Third Journey

Philippi;
Ruins of the ancient
city in northern
Greece. Paul visited
the city during his
first mission trip and
was imprisoned.

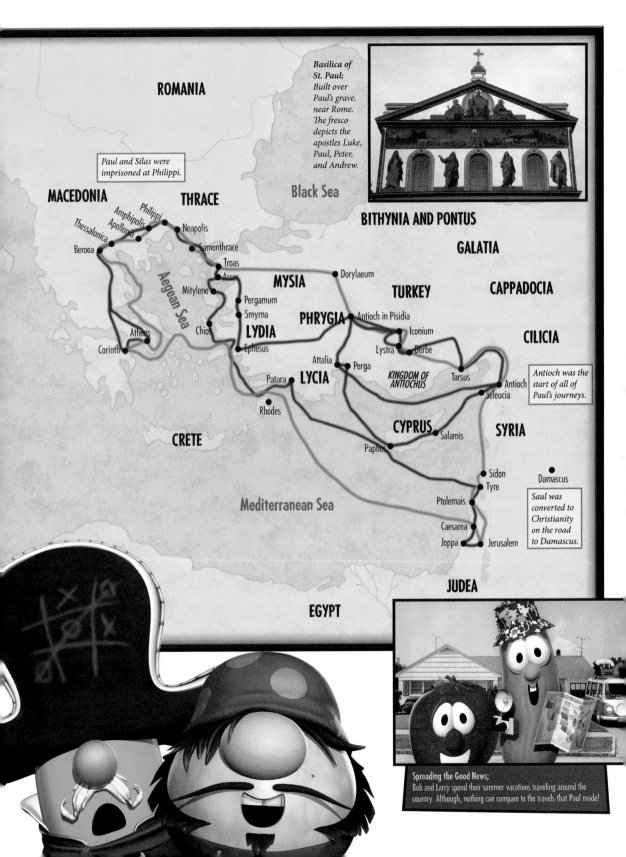

ROMANIA

Basilica of St. Paul; Built over Paul's grave, near Rome. The fresco depicts the apostles Luke, Paul, Peter, and Andrew.

Paul and Silas were imprisoned at Philippi.

Black Sea

MACEDONIA

THRACE

BITHYNIA AND PONTUS

GALATIA

Philippi
Amphipolis
Thessalonica
Apollonia
Beroea
Neapolis
Samonthrace
Troas
Assos
Mitylene
Chios

Aegean Sea

MYSIA

Dorylaeum

TURKEY

CAPPADOCIA

Pergamum
Smyrna

PHRYGIA

Antioch in Pisidia

Athens
Corinth

LYDIA

Ephesus

Attalia

Iconium
Lystra
Derbe

CILICIA

Perga

KINGDOM OF
ANTIOCHUS

Tarsus

Antioch was the start of all of Paul's journeys.

Patara

LYCIA

Antioch
Seleucia

Rhodes

CYPRUS

Salamis

SYRIA

CRETE

Paphos

Sidon
Tyre

Damascus

Mediterranean Sea

Ptolemais

Caesarea
Joppa
Jerusalem

Saul was converted to Christianity on the road to Damascus.

JUDEA

EGYPT

Spreading the Good News;
Bob and Larry spend their summer vacations traveling around the country. Although, nothing can compare to the travels that Paul made!

SPREAD OF CHRISTIANITY

Cologne
Trier
Rhine River
Rhone River
Lyons
Vienne
ITALY
Adriatic S
CORSICA
SARDINIA
Rome

Paul wrote to the Romans before visiting them in Rome.

Puteoli
SICILY
Carthage
Syracu
Cirta
AFRICA

Christianity had spread throughout much of the Roman Empire by the end of the first century A.D. The early apostles traveled to many lands telling others about Jesus, helping them to believe in him. Paul and John visited Asia Minor, Peter worked in Rome, Mark witnessed in Alexandria, Thomas spoke in India, and Thaddeus helped spread the gospel in Mesopotamia. This new Christian community was sometimes persecuted, but they held firm in their faith and the church grew.

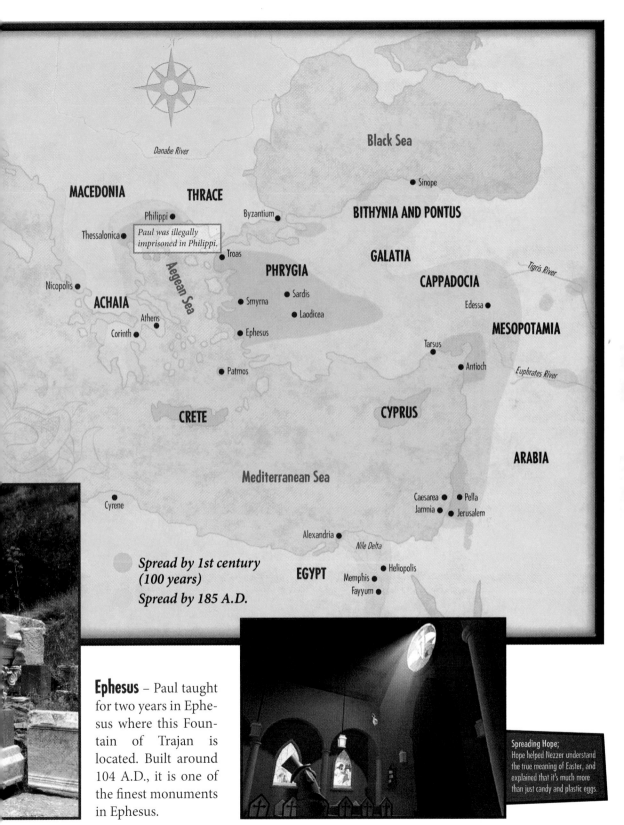

Danabe River

Black Sea

MACEDONIA

THRACE

Sinope

Philippi

Byzantium

BITHYNIA AND PONTUS

Thessalonica

Paul was illegally imprisoned in Philippi.

Troas

GALATIA

Tigris River

Aegean Sea

PHRYGIA

CAPPADOCIA

Nicopolis

Sardis

Edessa

ACHAIA

Smyrna

MESOPOTAMIA

Athens

Laodicea

Corinth

Ephesus

Tarsus

Patmos

Antioch

Euphrates River

CRETE

CYPRUS

ARABIA

Mediterranean Sea

Caesarea ● ● Pella
Jamnia ● ● Jerusalem

Cyrene

Alexandria

Nile Delta

Spread by 1st century (100 years)
Spread by 185 A.D.

EGYPT

Heliopolis

Memphis

Fayyum

Ephesus – Paul taught for two years in Ephesus where this Fountain of Trajan is located. Built around 104 A.D., it is one of the finest monuments in Ephesus.

THE HOLY LAND

The Holy Land holds a lot of religious importance. Archaeologists have found remains of the first and second temple and remains of the kingdoms of David and Solomon. The Holy Land is also home to the city of Jerusalem — where Jesus often taught and where he was crucified and put in a tomb, only to rise again. The city of Bethlehem, where Jesus was born, and the city of Nazareth, where Jesus lived and performed many miracles, are also part of this special territory. For over three thousand years, Jews have claimed Israel as their home, both as a sacred land and as a promised land.

The Damascus Gate;
Jerusalem's largest gate into the old city. Built where the Roman gate stood.

Jerusalem;
A view to the east. Jesus spoke on the Mount of Olives, which is in the background.
The Temple Mount with the golden dome of the Dome of the Rock is in the center.

LEBANON

Tyre

Caesarea Philippi

Mediterranean Sea

Hazor

SYRIA

Capernaum

Sea of Galilee

Cana

Nazareth

Shunem

Endor

Megiddo

Jezreel

Beth-Shean

Caesarea

Samaria

Shechem

Jordan River

Succoth

WEST BANK

Joppa

Shiloh

Adam

Ramah
(Arimathea)

Lydda

Rabbah

Bethel

Ai

Gilgal

JORDAN

Gibeon

Jericho

Ekron

Timnah

Emmaus

Bethany

Jerusalem

Ashdod

Gath

Bethlehem

Dead Sea

Lachish

Mamre

Hebron

Carmel

ISRAEL

Masada

Beersheba

NEGEV DESERT

Crusader Bazar;
Built in Jerusalem by the crusaders,
10th - 11th century A.D.

Searching for the Promised Land;
Josh and the Israelites set out to find the Promised Land.